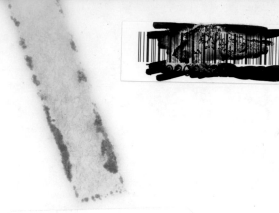

D0712922

Play and Interplay

A Manifesto for
New Design in Urban
Recreational Environment
by M. Paul Friedberg
with Ellen Perry Berkeley
Introduction by Thomas P. F. Hoving

The Macmillan Company
Collier-Macmillan Ltd., London

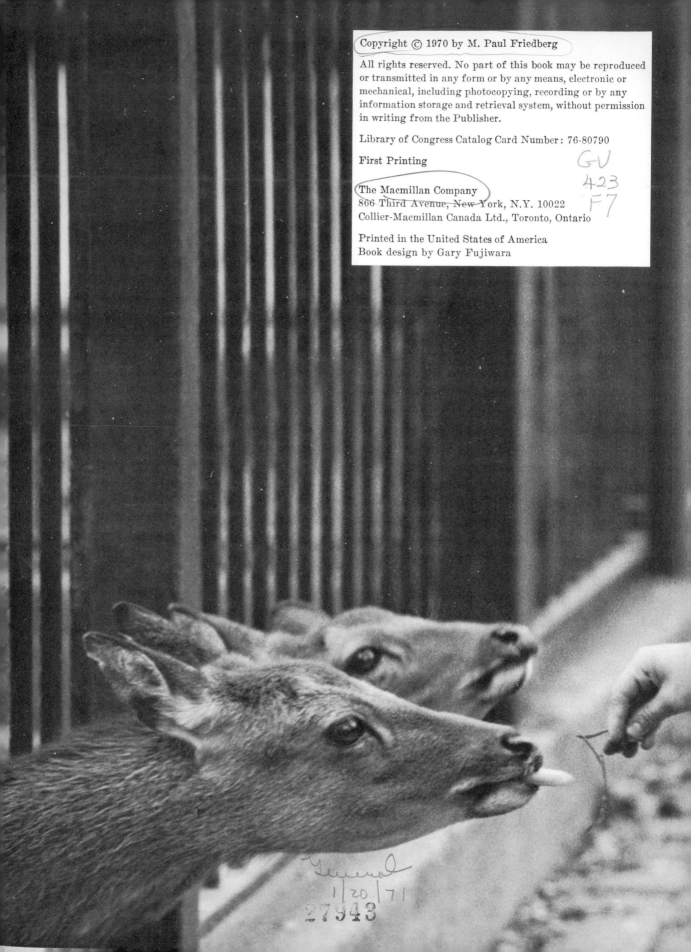

Library of Congress Catalog Card Number: 76-80790

First Printing

The Macmillan Company
866 Third Avenue, New York, N.Y. 10022
Collier-Macmillan Canada Ltd., Toronto, Ontario

Printed in the United States of America
Book design by Gary Fujiwara

To my wife Esther

All photographs were taken by the author except for the following: David Aaron, 23, 26–27, 29 (inset), 79; Martin Andrew, 184; Roy Berkeley, 60–61; Brian Burr, 188–189; Louis Chickman, 190–191; Educational Services, Inc., 82–83; Morton R. Engelberg, 131, 144–145; David Hirsch, 2–3, 42, 43, 50–51, 64–65, 67, 74–75, 76 (inset), 84, 102, 103, 108, 156, 157, 166, 170, 171 and inset, 172–173 and inset, 174–175, 176–177 and inset, 178–179 and inset, 182–183 and inset; William Mackey, 20–21, 53, 128; M. De Nalovy-Rozvadovski, 159, 186–187; The New York Times, 89 (inset); Katrina Thomas, 54–55, 86 (inset). Architects for four of the projects, Carver Houses, Riis Houses, Buchanan School, and Riis-Tompkins Link, were Pomerance and Breines.

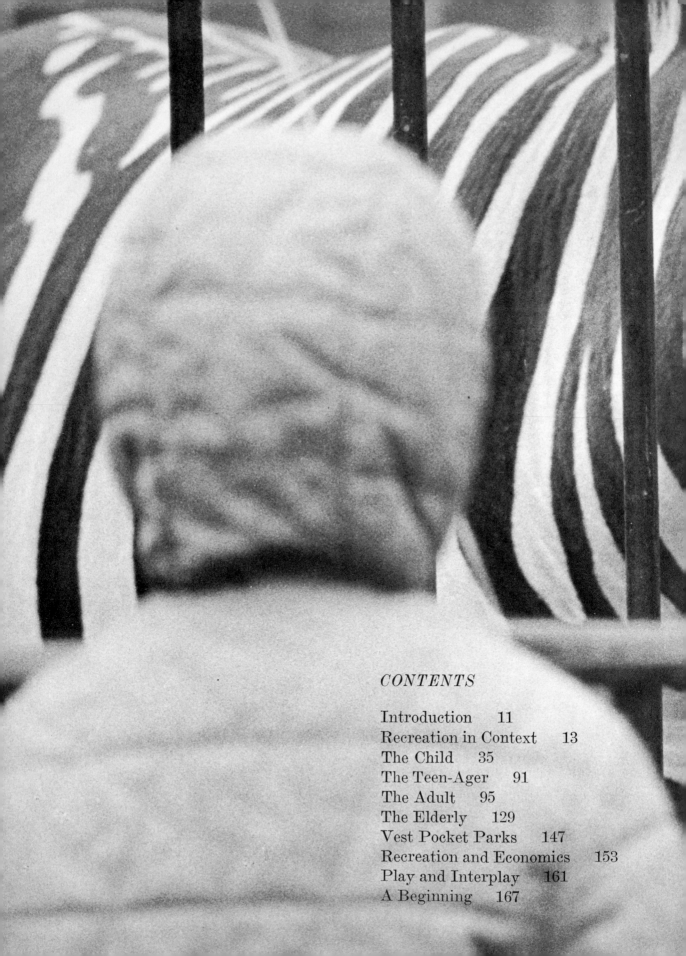

CONTENTS

Introduction

by Thomas P. F. Hoving

This is a courageous book. It takes courage to do battle with the existing way of doing things and to propose new ways as a replacement. On almost every page there is a challenge to the current procedures and the woeful product resulting from them. They deserve to be challenged. As Friedberg so aptly puts it, the common practice today is to consider recreation in terms of left-over time and left-over spaces. After reading this book, it is not possible to feel complacent about the left-overs that urban America serves up in the name of play.

But this is not a book that just tears down. It establishes a whole new way of looking at the complicated business of play, and shows that its very complexity and its different meaning for people of different ages is a source of new ideas.

Some of these new ideas have already been realized, and some of the innovative environments designed by Paul Friedberg are pictured on the following pages. (Not all of his ideas are for children, by any means, which will sur-prise people who think of Friedberg primarily for his well-known playgrounds.) Here are projects that go far beyond the description "playground" to encompass recreation for all ages and even, in the Harlem River project, buildings for all activities.

It takes wisdom to realize that the work of recreation does not depend entirely on the work of the designer. There are many other forces—social, economic, political—that can achieve as much as a physical design, or even more. This experience was brought home to me most clearly when I was Commissioner of Parks in New York City. Simply by closing streets in the park to traffic, we saw the already magnificent resource of Central Park become even more alive. Not a penny was spent; only the priorities and the rules were changed, as they should have been—after all, priorities are often outdated the day they are set and rules too frequently are merely cover-ups for what cannot be explained.

Often, too, it is not a question of new facilities but of looking with a fresh eye at what already exists. Central Park's placid Bethesda Fountain was successfully transformed into a place where a variety of people are in active "interplay"—eating, walking, singing, looking. This is one example from my own experience where a small outlay of funds has brought back an enormous return, both in money and in that richness of experience considered the essence of urban life.

This book also recognizes the vital importance of lively programming for urban parks and open spaces. Without creative events and activities to bring people together, the most imaginative physical plan can fail. The physical designer cannot plan it all ahead of time, and Paul Friedberg is quick to appreciate the added value when a park or street or plaza is put to creative use. He talks about the interplay between the design and what happens in it. One sees in his work that if the designer has asked the right questions and answered them, and if those responsible for carrying out interesting programs are alive to new possibilities, there is a *chance* (never a guarantee) that some memorable times may occur.

Incentives given to the private sector of the economy will undoubtedly be an important technique in getting better facilities and better programs for urban parks. As we all know, public budgets are stretched taut, and recreation is too often near the bottom of the list of essentials. This book has important ideas for the person in public or private capacity who is interested in making his city better and is open to new techniques in planning and administration.

I found it takes a different kind of courage and sensitivity in permitting those who will use a park to have a role in the design of that park. A great deal has been said, recently, about whether nonprofessional people should join in this process of design, and if so, how. Friedberg's comments about how a vest pocket park can be built and what it can mean for a neighborhood will be helpful to those who are concerned lest even something as small as a vest pocket park become one more item imposed on a community because someone outside thought it would be good for them.

Let me suggest that children, too, can and ultimately should be designers of the playground, bringing things from home or digging into a heap of things provided by the designer. This book reflects many such ideas—courageous ideas that have not yet had a reasonable trial and are therefore not yet a safe bet. But safe bets shouldn't always get top priority. We need tough-minded and realistic views about how to handle a child's natural need for challenge. We need experimentation and imagination.

Perhaps the ultimate courage, though, was for the author (admirably aided by the lively prose of Ellen Berkeley) to document this on paper. As he admits, these thoughts are in process of refinement and development. Hopefully, the rapid experimentation apparent in his work over the past decade will continue and accelerate. I am sure that Paul Friedberg would be happy to see this book take its place some day as an early, and perhaps quaint, pioneering expression of the new way of thinking.

The cities today have many problems. Recreation is, simultaneously, one of those problems and a way to alleviate many of the other problems. My philosophy—that through open space, people can become more aware of each other, more responsive to each other, more fully developed as human beings— clearly parallels attitudes illustrated and delineated in this book. At a time when many persons feel that cities are no longer any good or any fun, this readable volume carries a message of hopefulness and commitment.

Recreation in Context

This is not another book about recreation and open space, about how to design parks, playgrounds, and plazas. The reader will find no data on the proper distance between swings for a given area of playground, or the proper number of basketball courts for a given size of population.

True, this is a book about recreation. But it is about a new recreation, explored in a new context. If the exploration suggests (as it does) that more swings as we know them will not answer the recreational needs of the child, any subsequent discussion on the distance between swings becomes absurd. So if you are in possession of some swings and want to know how to locate them in relation to one another or in relation to a larger area, do not look for help in the following pages. This is not a manual for constructing new facilities but a

volume to shake loose old ideas. If, after finishing the book, you decide to unload your swings on someone who has not yet taken this volume home with him, we wish you every success.

Another caution: the exploration will proceed more by compass than by road map, seeking new directions in general, rather than precise routes to specific places. If, after digesting this volume, you decide that your existing basketball court is deficient and needs redesign, or that the teen-agers need an entirely new recreational place, we wish you well but offer no precise rules for the design.

The Urban Setting

The focus of the book is recreation in the urban environment. A state park forty miles outside the city is undeniably attractive but cannot be considered the primary recreational possibility for city residents; the metropolitan park should be regarded, instead, as a supplement to what the city already offers. Obviously a large park outside the heavily urbanized area offers things that the central city cannot. But recreation is not to be equated with vast open space. Recreational needs can, and must, be met in the densely built-up areas of the strictly urban setting.

Unfortunately, most cities offer a largely inadequate place for recreation. A few city dwellers are able to sidestep the deficiency by having second homes, joining country clubs, taking vacation trips, and sending their children to summer camps. But these alternatives are not feasible for the majority. The contention of this book is that a city within

13

its boundaries must be able to handle the recreational needs of all its citizens.

This book is therefore directed primarily to the recreational needs of those who can't get out of the city (or don't want to)—who are limited in time, energy, funds, or transportation, or who otherwise want to enjoy themselves close to home. These are the people who don't have a private terrace or private club (or even a satisfactory apartment) at their disposal; they are thrown on the public environment for much of their leisure time. This is the sidewalk and fire-escape scene, where women enjoy their free time gossiping at the market, where men drink beer on the front stoop or play dominoes at a portable bridge table on the sidewalk, where children play hopscotch (in between passing cars) in the street, and where the older people lean out over a gritty window ledge to experience it all vicariously.

New Answers Are Needed

Recreation will not solve the important social and economic problems of our time. Recreation is, in fact, trivial compared to the problems of unemployment, bad housing, hunger, disease, racism, and war. But we are heading toward a time in this country when recreation will be one of our main occupations. As the work week grows shorter, the leisure week will expand to fill the time. And we will be no better for the lessening of burdensome or boring work if our leisure is only another burden and bore. Already there are growing numbers of people in the cities spending growing amounts of leisure time in an environment that has rapidly become less livable and less fun. New answers are needed.

Thus far not even the most recreationally enlightened cities have begun to create a real recreational environment, because they suffer from the universal preconception that recreation consists of "facilities." Unquestionably, in areas where there are few facilities the more of them the better, but this is not the whole answer. Even a thousand new basketball courts, each surrounded by its chain-link fencing, will not answer the needs of the urban teen-ager; more basketball courts will probably produce better basketball players but will not make for a better recreational life for this age group.

Cities are creating facilities today that don't respond to more than the smallest of our needs; the procedure is

to provide this facility or that one without evaluating people's true needs, habits, nature, and desires. People are expected to be overwhelmingly grateful at receiving *any* new facility; they play their part, and the procedure goes unchallenged.

In the old days of radio, so the story goes, when the Firestone Hour was a well-loved program, Mr. Firestone was approached with the idea of moving the program to a new time so that more people could hear it. Sunday afternoon at three was suggested. "Nonsense," said Mr. Firestone, "everyone will be out playing polo then!" How many of our recreational "experts" today—public administrators, playground designers, equipment manufacturers, educators—are operating under comparable delusions about recreation.

The Impact of Environment

The "facility" approach serves only a fragment of a full recreational life. Recreation is not a fenced-off part of our lives, just as education does not occur only in a school. But recreation will become more and more fragmented—less and less recreational—unless we evaluate its meaning for people, evaluating whether their needs are fulfilled or thwarted by their whole environment. Satisfying these needs will involve more than the occasional (or even frequent) use of a "facility." It will require an environment that is beneficial—re-creational—to the whole man. The effects of the urban environment today, however, are probably more pervasive (and less beneficial) than the effects of any time

spent in "recreation"; the urban environment has the power to desensitize the perceptions, cause an unnecessary physical strain, create a lingering disorientation, intensify a growing apathy and lack of involvement, limit the capacity to communicate with others, reduce the ability to learn and develop. The environment batters us so devastatingly that no number of basketball games or picnics or bowling matches can neutralize the impact.

"Environment" is a much-used word, and because it is a concept so important to the ideas in this volume, it would be well to give it specific connotation. The environment (and this book considers only the public environment) can be described as the sum of what we meet when we go out into the world—the bricks and mortar, the sounds and smells, the spaces, the systems (such as transportation), the sights (such as light in the sky or neon along the streets)—in short, all the things that make up our surroundings. An aura is part of the public environment (a feeling of hurry or ease); the microscopic pollutants in the atmosphere are part of the public environment. Essentially, then, it is what we can see and feel with our senses, not just with our five senses but with our sixth, as well, and with our varied capacities (those still unbattered) for delight or excitement or mystery or peace.

Walt Whitman wrote: "There was a child went forth every day, and the first object he looked upon and received with wonder, pity, love, or dread, that object he became. Part of him for the day, or a certain part of day, or for many years, 15 or stretching cycles of years." Everything that exists in our environment has the power to have some effect on some part of us.

To see the relationship between the "facility" and the whole recreational environment, one has only to think of the many parks that are bordered by a polluted river on one side and the dangerous barrier of a "parkway" on the other. At night, when the park might be most desirable to working people, these unattractive features (plus the fear of muggers or worse) combine to keep it relatively empty. The environment defeats the facility. And one has only to think of the many playgrounds to which the toddler must be led by the hand, across streets choked with cars. The child must then be caged in the playground like an animal in a zoo for fear he will wander off into the street. Even if the facility were attractive in itself (which is not usually the case, with fence-to-fence asphalt carpeting and the deadly lines of those metal baby-sitters we call swings), its environmental context is abrasive. While the child would probably prefer being *outside* the playground in the street, sailing debris down rivulets in a gutter, the urban environment—despite its liveliness and interest—is essentially hostile. The environment detracts from the facility.

The environment is not the same for all age groups. The preschool child is taken by the hand on his limited travels near his home; his public environment is primarily the stoop, the sidewalk, the street, the little park. When he goes to school, he has a whole new environment, perhaps five to ten blocks in diameter.

The teen-ager's environment is broader still; the adult's is the entire city; and the elderly person's is again relatively restricted, his lessened mobility keeping him near home.

To overlook the environment and think only of "facilities" is to embroider on a worn fabric. Consider the preschool child. He should not have to cross vehicular streets on his way to a neighborhood park; the streets should be pedestrian ways, or perhaps the street should *become* the park. Or consider the elderly who spend their time sitting on the traffic islands of Upper Broadway, filling their eyes with the people who pass by, their lungs with the fumes from cars, trucks, and buses. The city is planning to prettify these islands, but the improvement can hardly be considered an improvement in the recreational environment of the elderly. Their need is not for a few fume-drenched plants on these depressing slivers of real estate; their need is for active places of enriched experience where they can be with people, watch people, and feel that they are still part of society.

Does planting answer any of the real needs that send the lonely elderly out onto the traffic islands? They are like the man in the story who has lost his key in a dark hallway. A friend sees him looking for it and asks him where he dropped it. "Over there," is the reply. "Then why are you down on the floor over *here*?" the friend asks. "Because this is where the light is." We can easily plant and beautify and design new graphics, because people understand this kind of tangible improvement. It is easy to understand a specific program—so many trees, of so many different types, planted under certain conditions, and so on. It is harder to question whether a tree is the most important improvement that we can make. So we take the easy way out and find ourselves prettifying a system that is inadequate in ways that tree planting cannot remedy. We are looking for the key in the wrong corner of the hallway.

Perhaps city government is simply not geared to handling the larger questions. The recreational environment of every city is fragmented among many different departments—parks, recreation, open space, zoning, planning, building, highway, education, and so on. Each department operates largely by responding to the pressures of the moment instead of looking at the larger needs. The city consistently overlooks the forest for the tree planting.

Change and Experimentation

This book does not accept the existing rules as inevitable. It seeks to analyze recreational needs and possibilities without reference to the prevailing orientation toward "facilities." The aim is to induce change from this orientation and to encourage change as a continuing response to the unforeseen situations of the decades ahead. Experimentation and exploration should continue, by a process of trial and error, in much the same way that a person continues to develop: learning from what has gone before and being open to what has never been tried.

Recreational planning has usually operated with leftover spaces, leftover money, and leftover ideas. It is time to look at the whole subject with as few preconceptions as possible. The exploration must also be as comprehensive as possible; it is past time when problems can be considered one at a time. Recreation planning has usually destroyed positive values because it has considered only one-dimensional situations and posed one-dimensional solutions. Recreation is very much a part of the total planning process and should be integrated with education, housing, commerce and transportation. To exclude recreation from the initial planning is to reduce its impact.

"Progress" in the technological and material sense has come to mean that the environment becomes steadily more offensive, more deleterious to the enjoyment of human pleasures. The challenge in our urban environment is to use our resources to open recreational possibilities that are truly re-creational, that heighten experience and increase enjoyment for all urban dwellers and for all their lives.

The country—an environment of life, texture, and richness; clean, healthful, and beneficient.

The city—an environment of contrasts and contradictions; crowded, noisy, and dirty; exciting, active, and vital—a dynamic world of richness and complexity.

The child is a product of his environment. No one design can meaningfully apply to his different needs and experiences.

Interplay between the object and the child makes his total world—play. He exploits the vitality of his environment and draws upon his imagination to create his world.

The street—spontaneous, exciting, and immediate—competes with home, school, and playground for the possession of the child. The street wins hands down.

Playgrounds that deny the child; that offer no chance of involvement, participation, or manipulation; that are devoid of choice, complexity, and interaction will be empty of children— a dead ground. The street will be the playground.

Complexity offers alternatives and choice and the tools of the growth process. Psychologists tell us that rich environments make for healthy personalities. Limit the environment and you limit the man.

The Child

Play is the child's work. The world is his laboratory, and he is its scientist. Play is the research by which he explores himself and his relationship to the world.

Childhood—with its work and play inseparable—is a time for nurturing intellect and molding personality, for developing potentialities, for discovering life and experiencing it. Limit the experience and the child is limited; limit the child and the adult is limited. The child is truly father of the man.

We have discovered the awesomeness of this truth only in recent years. We know now that the creative mind stultified during its greatest developmental period can never make up for the loss. If the learning process is thwarted during the earliest years, the child and the man will be forever stunted. We know, too, that the child does half his learning before he is four years old, another 30 per cent before he is eight, and only 20 per cent during the remaining years of elementary and secondary education. And during the years that learning capacity is being forged, a child spends as much time at play—in and out of the playground—as in the classroom.

How does a child learn? He learns by doing, and much of what he learns is through play. Most of what he learns is not conscious or intellectual but comes from physical involvement as he tests his developing skills and powers against new challenges. Environment is vitally important. Balancing out the previous swing of the pendulum toward heredity, psychologists now consider environment a major factor in learning. Recent experiments show that children respond directly to an enriched environment, developing their awarenesses and capabilities at a geometric rate when the environment is a stimulating one.

With demonstrable gain in the offing, and irreparable loss by default, it becomes unthinkable not to strive for a more exciting and enriching environment for children. Even without the positive results for the future, the sheer enjoyment for the present is reason enough.

Play as a Continual Process

But the prevailing notion of play takes little cognizance of the potentialities either for joy or for growth. To many adults, play is only a holding action, a leftover time during which a child must be kept busy and out of mischief. Just as TV becomes an electronic baby-sitter, so do our existing play facilities become great, gray outdoor nannies, incarcerating children and protecting them from experience and involvement. The air may be fresh, but the play is stale, and many children are saying exactly this when they escape the confines of a dull playground to play in a nearby gutter, street, or empty lot. There is no contest between the richness outside the playground—color, movement, people, life— and the dreariness of the standard playground trio—swing, slide, and seesaw.

Most adults do not yet understand that a child plays without waiting for specific times or places to play. We find it hard to remember that play and learning are a continual and integrated process. We try to fragment the child's life —a time to play, a time to learn, a time to rest. The child doesn't recognize a special time to play, though; his whole world is an adventure. It is adults who punctuate the day with "proper" times for play (usually not adequate) and punctuate the city with "proper" areas for play (usually not appropriate).

Archaic Equipment

A walk through almost any city will verify the extent of the problem. Play equipment is archaic and sentimental, dropped into sterile plains of asphalt, bounded by forbidding fences (to keep people out, or in?). This environment is worse than neutral; it is negative and therefore ultimately destructive of development. Even the most "advantaged" children today—their homes stocked with toys, their parents providing constant outlets into the world— suffer from the deficiencies of the public environment. Those whose financial resources are minimal—whose level of experience is lower, whose housing is cramped, whose neighborhood is dilapidated—have the more urgent need for a decent and stimulating public environment, but it is safe to say that the entire childhood population, rich and poor, is in need of a more meaningful outdoor environment.

Play facilities are uniformly dreary because of a combination of factors— apathy, misconception of children's needs, lack of reasonable alternatives as models, and an exaggerated emphasis on the management and maintenance of facilities. Lady Allen of Hurtwood, a landscape architect in England who has championed the rough and tumble "adventure playgrounds" (where children build caves and cabins out of leftover materials dumped onto the site), has said that American playgrounds are designed for the insurance companies. Obviously, playgrounds are not being designed for the child.

Questioning the Stereotypes

Contrary to popular opinion, the playground is not an easy design problem. Because it is an appealing area of design and one that doesn't require special credentials (people also raise children without special experience), anyone feels he can design play facilities. However, the real challenge is not just to give the child something to play with (he can play with a stick and be happy with it) but to make the play experience meaningful. The professional designer will make a successful playground only if he has a solid knowledge of children's behavior; the social, psychological physical patterns of behavior are the essential springboard for his design. The designer can no longer simply purchase the manufactured equipment that is currently available (although the solution ultimately is for designers to work closely with manufacturers). Nor can he simply borrow another designer's vocabulary—in effect, using the idiom without understanding the language—and hope to have a total environment that is significant in its own right.

Preconceptions that the traditional swing, slide, and seesaw provide a desirable play experience must be questioned. Each of these traditional pieces creates no more than a one-dimensional play experience, and with it a one-dimensional child. However, an important distinction is necessary. To question this stereotyped playground equipment is not to deny the *activities* provided by them; the swinging, sliding, and balancing they provide are natural loves of every child. The challenge is to provide these activities in a way that does not automatically set up a single predetermined and limited pattern.

Research and Evaluation

Preconceptions about children's genuine play patterns can be demolished only by research. Expensive equipment is not required, since the best place to study the child is in a natural setting, where he is free to explore anything, natural or man-made, and is not constrained by the configurations of specific "equipment." He may climb a tree or throw a rope over a branch for a swing or jump from a rock or find water, sand, or tree branches to play with. Or build things. Or demolish things. When the world is open to him, his imagination puts it to good use.

If we see what a child makes of his environment when there are few constraints, we can bring new possibilities into the urban play environment, working them in with what we already know from other avenues of research about childhood learning and development. The aim is a multifaceted environment, existing on physical, social, and educational levels and suited to the child who can develop, through play, on all these levels at once. (Do we want the kind of children who are content with the asphalt-dreary playground and its standard swings and slides?)

Unfortunately such research is rare. It is easier to justify research for the sick, retarded, or disturbed child than for the "normal" one. Evaluation of existing play designs is also rare. But children are not all the same; they vary according to income level, ethnic group, and high-rise/low-rise living. Shouldn't it be important to know which ideas work, in which ways, and for whom? Typically, the little evaluation of design that is done is a seat-of-the-pants operation and suffers from several defects. When a play piece is new, it may be dangerously overused, and if accidents take place, the timid bureaucrat finds it easier to remove the item (and pronounce it a failure) than to evaluate the problem and modify accordingly. Also, since much playground equipment is fastened irrevocably together, it is usually easier to remove the entire piece than to improve it. To be worthwhile, evaluation must continue over a long period of time and include modifications of design during the process.

Any research is inevitably met by resistance to change. The bureaucrat will resist change, having an unwillingness to take risks or learn new ways; the manufacturer will also resist change, having an investment in expensive machinery that is already producing a marketable product. Actually, the manufacturers should put up a good deal of the money for research; they will have to face the risks of changing their designs, but they will also benefit from increased sales. It is unthinkable that they should continue to foist on the public the present collection of inadequate designs. The traditional slide is virtually fifty years old; it is startling that so few buyers question its adequacy.

Developing an Attitude

The climate of design began to change only several years ago, with increasing pressure from parents and educators, and increasing support from foundations. During these few years, M. Paul Friedberg & Associates has had the opportunity to build a series of playgrounds, and—through them—to engage in a unique experimental program. These particular playgrounds were not funded by the government and therefore were built quickly, without the usual two- and three-year time lag between design conception and completion. We were able to see an immediate response to one playground while we were in the process of designing the next.

Responsibility for playground design has usually fallen to the landscape archi-tect. However, because of his limited schooling in the subject (the professional schools are as guilty of preconceptions as anyone else), and because of the lack of a medium for accumulating information on playground design, it was usually easier to take the word of the manufacturers on what constituted a good playground. Originally, then, like almost everyone else, we considered play areas a stepchild, and we accepted catalog searches as the inevitable technique of design. From catalogs, we selected the specified number of slides, swings, seesaws. The very nature of this equipment demands that each piece be isolated. Swings are barricaded because they are dangerous to others. Sandboxes are segregated because the principle has been so wholeheartedly accepted by clients (many of them in maintenance-oriented park departments) and so little questioned by users (many of them not yet at the level of coherent speech). Playgrounds were, and often still are, no more imaginatively designed than public toilets—so many fixtures, so many feet between them, floor surfacing of such-and-such, and that's that.

It wasn't long before we were dissatisfied with this approach, and at least began searching through a different kind of catalog. Manufacturers were just beginning to make what are now called "contemporary pieces"—the concrete turtles, bears, and porpoises that have become domesticated in many parks and housing projects over the past decade. We chose what we *thought* children would like, not remembering what *we* had really liked ourselves when we were children. The search was for the best-looking turtle, the best-looking bear. The animals are pleasant enough and have reasonable play value for a short time but ultimately have no lasting play value for the normal child with a lively imagination and short attention span. Actually, these "play sculptures" are neither fish nor fowl; they are not suitable as play pieces and they do not make the grade as sculpture, as an artist's comment on his world. Both aspects suffer from the demand to combine them, and the child does not respond to the piece either as a play item or a work of art.

"Play sculpture" is difficult for the designer to use, too. Each of these animals demands its own territory as if it were a real animal. We have tried to use them as focal points, as if they were truly sculptural, but they aren't sculp-

ture, and they don't stand alone with any substantial esthetic power. They are almost impossible to integrate with other play pieces. Perhaps the only successful combination is the mating of one turtle with another turtle; this has a biological tidiness but suffers from the same esthetic limitation. A playground with even the best of these contemporary animals is still an area with its equipment not fully integrated into the visual landscape; it is not yet an environment.

Carver: First of a Series

In 1963 we were asked by the Astor Foundation to remodel the outdoor spaces at Carver Houses, an existing public housing project between Park and Madison avenues, from 99th to 103rd Streets, in New York City. The area already had a small playground, asphalted to continue an adjacent walkway and enclosed by a chain-link fence four feet high. In the playground were an arched climber, a painted hopscotch, and a make-believe stoop for stoop ball. (This stoop was a beginning step but a misdirected one. The child develops games like stoop ball or stick ball from his environmental context, using manhole covers as stick ball bases because they exist ready-made for the purpose. But an isolated manhole cover designed into a playground would be meaningless, and the artificial stoop, alone, is similarly devoid of its original meaning.) In our remodeling, we developed a spray pool with seals, frogs, and turtles; we relocated the arched climber and added a sandbox. None of this was creative, however. The design is pleas- *39* ant but essentially lacking in play possibilities. With large crowds, it is exciting because of the people; without people, it is dull for the child.

140th Street: A Further Step

Then we had the opportunity to revise a playground we had designed two years earlier (it hadn't yet been built) for a housing project on 140th Street in Manhattan. The site was exciting, with many rock outcroppings and a slope that fell away eight to ten feet. It became obvious to us that if the playground were flattened, its potential for excitement would be severely flattened too. Our first change in the proposed design, therefore, was to add terraced steps, accommodating the design to the gradient, and to add a series of concrete bollards at various levels; older children could use them for jumping, and younger ones could walk through them like a maze. We built a slide that could be approached from 180 degrees along wide steps (regulations of the state housing authority prohibit movable equipment like the standard swing). We still had not been weaned away from the manufacturers, although by this time we had found a new line that seemed different. (It wasn't.)

We discovered during construction that the potentiality for play existed in the land forms as much as—and more than—in the man-made line. The children were playing all over the steps during the rebuilding, enjoying themselves then and afterward with more enthusiasm than they showed later with the space ship and "trees" from the manufacturer. When the manufactured

play pieces were put into place, they almost destroyed what had been a handsome space, a simple series of geometric forms. They were in conflict with the over-all design and in conflict with one another. In addition, they were static pieces, offering static experiences. Every adult said it was a fine playground, but we were beginning to be aware that we knew very little about children's play. And we regretted the expense of these concrete "sculptures," which seemed doubly expensive in terms of the limited play experience they provided. The major expense of the playground, however, was for surfacing, fencing, and wall— none of these for play!

The Role of Manufactured Items

Obviously, manufactured items are not all bad. Some play pieces are sensitively

designed and extremely valuable. The geodesic dome, for instance, has enormous potential. Some pieces, too, work well enough in certain situations. The difficulty is not that the equipment is manufactured but that it produces predetermined patterns and movements as a result of its design, and unrelated and limited experiences as a result of its necessary isolation.

It is obvious, too, that the designer should work with the manufacturer to develop design elements with better play value. A modular system is a natural result of collaboration between manufacturer and designer. Very much like the single brick, the module is only a starting point; modular design of play facilities allows the designer to create an unlimited variety of play forms from a single well-designed module. A child

can play on and through the total form, on his route from one experience to the next. The masses and voids created by the assembly of modules are as important in play as are the more obvious experiences with rope swings, slide poles, etc., that may be part of the total form.

Straus: The Next Attempt

While the 140th Street playground was being built, the design for the Nathan Straus housing project, also in New York City, was in progress. Here we worked in a very limited way with a manufacturer's modular item—the climbing ring—and related it to concrete pods. The composition was harmonious and interesting, and we were pleased to find a standard item that could be inexpensively worked into a design situation. But the design encountered difficulty on another level. When the play area was first opened, it was extensively used; the children had almost nowhere to play until then, and they went berserk. The high initial use, and the mixture of age groups, led to some accidents—specifically on the small landing pods. The Housing Authority suggested lowering the pods; we doubted that this would solve the problem and suggested making the landing pods larger. The Housing Authority was unwilling to do so, and eventually public pressure caused the pods to be removed altogether. (We have since used the design successfully elsewhere, using wider pods and putting two pods together for a larger landing place.)

Riis: A Total Play Environment

Then at Riis Houses, from Avenue D

to the East River Drive, 6th to 10th Streets, Manhattan, we attempted our first total play environment. (Again the Astor Foundation was the enlightened client.) Here we wanted to provide for all activities in a unified design. We analyzed what activities we wanted, or didn't want (no running, for instance, since collisions rather than falls are the major causes of injuries in playgrounds). We then created experiences comparable to those a child might find elsewhere in widely scattered areas—a mountain, a tunnel, a tree house—and brought these together into a single environment. The experiences are separated not by fences but by changes in level and by other subtleties of design. The result is a series of architectonic forms that have an organic relationship. Unity of material is a strong factor in the cohesiveness of the design; all the major forms are of granite block. Sand, wood, and concrete are interspersed throughout as secondary materials.

The granite forms keep the playground effectively clear of pedestrian traffic and make a boundary that is visual, not physical. This is definitely a child's world; the adult is a trespasser. But while the playground is a distinct area, it is not isolated from the surroundings. It is not a cage; it has no fences. The child can be seen from outside, which pleases him, and the adult can police the area from outside, which may prevent situations from getting out of hand. There are barriers, of a kind, since some control is needed for the intensity of play, but these barriers are not so much physical (chain-link fences) as tactile (changes in grade level to inhibit running and contain play). There are no signs; the area announces its varied possibilities to children simply by its inherent excitement.

At the back of the Riis playground, however, the Housing Authority insisted on a chain-link fence. Just inside the fence is a low concrete wall with a mural, marking the effective boundary of the play area. The children play naturally on the wall, but have no inclination to go beyond it into the three-foot walkway between wall and fence. If the wall were removed, the entire design would suffer, but if the *fence* were removed, the design would improve. Enclosure is important to keep children from running out suddenly, but it can often be implicit instead of explicit. Fencing should always be a design decision, not a functional decision alone.

The basic floor material at Riis is sand; there is no question that it requires more maintenance than asphalt, but we also know that young children require more maintenance than older ones. There is no objection to safety surfaces—rubberized asphalt, or pure rubber pads—but because they have little or no play value in themselves, sand is preferable. Safety surfacing is preferable to asphalt, if money permits. The fake grass (made of real plastic) is appealing: it sends out a strong "touch me" message. But why green? Why not blue or some other color? Materials like tanbark and natural earth are least successful; they retain moisture and are hard to clean. The richness of sand as a play material for all age groups made it the logical choice at Riis; the play area is, in effect, one large sandbox.

The granite mounds at Riis offer structures for the children to climb, run up, lie down on, and so forth, but the structures themselves are not complex enough to maintain interest. We therefore added to them for a system of *linked play.* These added facilities involve to a large extent the activities found in a traditional playground— sliding, balancing, swinging—but Riis features significant departures. The Riis slide is built into an igloo, providing a 360-degree access. There is further access from three tunnels, into the center, and up a ladder. The area at the top is flattened out so that children can rest, wait their turn, or simply look around from a better vantage point.

Various age groups use the igloo tunnels—as a maze, as a place to play tag, as access to the slide. During construction we were apprehensive about the tunnels, wondering what other uses ingenious children would find for them. Four gates were built and installed for night-time closing of the igloo, but the gates were almost immediately ripped off and never seen again. There has never been any "trouble" in the tunnels. There *have* been interesting occasions, however, as when some mattresses were brought into the tunnels and set afire, sending smoke billowing out of the top—a marvelous event in this "Don't Touch" world. Undoubtedly, too, there are sexual explorations carried out here, by preteens during the day, teens at night. I am reminded, here, of the concrete table that was provided in one small new park and was soon used intensively by local boys for gambling. The immediate response of the city was to remove the table! Did they imagine that gambling did not exist until the table appeared or that it would stop when the table was gone?

Children reach the large mound from other mounds, climbing over or hanging from various arched climbers. A child can traverse vast areas without touching the ground, which is an adventure in itself. One deficiency at Riis is the lack of moving equipment (swings), but the children solved this on their own by adding ropes to the arched climbers. Ideally it would be best to leave a playground unfinished, letting children bring their creative participation to it. But there are often difficulties in the children's lack of materials (their ropes were not strong enough) and in making enough materials available for such large groups.

The Concept of Linked Play

The most important advance at Riis was the development of *linked play,* through the juxtaposition of different elements and the ties between them. A child can climb up and down, go through a variety of experiences on any mound, and enjoy moving from one mound to the next. Path systems begin to be created, and reciprocal movements, so that when a child runs down one mound his momentum carries him up the next. The moving from one experience to the next is an experience in itself. The choice of what to do next becomes an experience. The more complex the playground, the greater the choice and the more enriched the learning experience. This kind of playground has richness for the child whether he is there for a single day or returns again and again. The concept of linked play provides play activity far beyond the number of play pieces employed in isolation. The quantity as well as the quality of play is enhanced. Links or bridges can be simple or sophisticated—plank, cable, rope, or manufactured items. Links shouldn't be so premeditated as to keep the child moving only in circles; diagonals should be possible—and culs-de-sac. But however he moves, he should feel a sense of continuity in the environment.

One segment of the Riis playground was designed as a maze. The young children use it as a maze, and the older ones climb over the top, but it has severe deficiencies as a play form. The real activity—the real focal point of the playground—is in the linked area, in a variety of routes. A child doesn't take long to discover that the maze doesn't "go anywhere"; it is not high enough to provide an exciting vantage point; and it does not lead to other activities. (It also does not have enough happening in it, no mirrors or rewards that are the fun of any traditional maze.)

In linked play, the child doesn't simply stand in the middle of a play area and decide to walk over and use a slide or swing. This is not spontaneous choice; the hiatus destroys spontaneity. A hiatus *is* permissible, however (and necessary), at the top of any of these play forms—at the top of a mound or tree house, for instance. These stopping points for "passive play" allow increased numbers in the playground without causing chaos, and allow the child a frequently needed rest period.

Adults may relegate children's play

to a special place or to the status of a minor activity. "Child's play" defines an activity as beneath serious attention. But to the child, play is as real as anything else he does. And it pervades his entire world. We expected children to play everywhere at Riis—among the sitting areas, in the great inverted mountain of the amphitheater, in the fountain—everywhere. The entire plaza has been designed with permissiveness. Nothing is fragile; the slats of the benches, for instance, are 4x4 timbers to defy destruction. (The scale is consistent throughout, and these oversized details are not noticed as such.) We knew children would go into the planting beds and again decided to accept the inevitable and deal with it by design. Thus the planting areas of the plaza are sprinkled with large wooden stepping

stones. These probably invite the children into the planting areas but also keep them off most of the greenery, and the result is that both plants and children can thrive.

Vest Pocket Parks: New Ideas

The next step in design development took place in the Bedford-Stuyvesant section of Brooklyn, in a situation that was the exact opposite of Riis; the site was of a smallness suitable for a vest pocket park and the budget was of a smallness possible to a neighborhood group. Since the site was already paved and we didn't want the expense of bringing back a paving contractor, the challenge was to design a play environment that would not require breaking the asphalt for foundations. We bolted together varying lengths of 12x12 timbers, making mounds up to six feet high and of sufficient weight and horizontal surface not to require footings and foundations. (The forms included pipes for varied design and play possibilities.)

It was interesting during construction to watch the children play on the large timbers that were brought to the site. This was the first construction that many of them had seen in their neighborhood, and their first direct involvement with construction materials; it was *our* first experience watching children improvise upon a design in progress. They would run along one timber, jump to another, or come to a dead stop when there was nowhere else to go. Play stopped when a gap was too wide to be bridged. We began to add bridges, by rearranging timbers, so that play could continue without interruption. The children were junior partners in the design, and the concept of linked play received an added input.

At Bedford-Stuyvesant, the standard lengths of timber, bolted together, made the forms not only easy to assemble but also easy to dismantle. The need for change is too pervasive to keep making unchanging and unchangeable playgrounds. There is a need to adapt to new ideas as they evolve from research; a need to respond to changing populations in a community; a need to correct initial faults of design; a need to provide a more varied experience for those who spend many years using only a single play area; and a need to utilize, even temporarily, sites that may be vacant for only a limited time.

The Modular Concept Expanded

Imagine being able, overnight, to have an entirely new playground. Under a federal grant, at this point, we had the opportunity to expand the modular concept of the changing environment. Here evolved four types of play equipment—three modular, one not—but none requiring foundations and each capable of being juxtaposed harmoniously into larger forms. The modular units are concrete U and J shapes, kept together by their own weight; tubular steel boxes, bolted together; and wood timbers (in standard lengths) stacked together. The nonmodular units are pipe-and-cable pieces.

The modular or standardized systems have great practical value in adapting to a site that is available for only a short period of time. Units can be brought in to utilize an empty lot almost overnight, and when the site is taken for another use the piece can be dismantled and reassembled on another site or returned temporarily to central storage. These factory-made pieces offer additional and considerable benefits in quality control and cost.

The module is only a basic building block with which the designer can create an unlimited variety of designs. Far from limiting him, the module frees him. The playground designer is now clearly more than a purchaser of "play sculpture." He is potentially the designer of a total environment that works in various ways and can be unlike any that has been created before.

Playgrounds of the Future

With the idea of change comes the idea of the child's doing the modification himself—the playground as a product *of* the child, not a ready-made design *for* the child. Every child needs to express himself and have an effect on his own environment; these needs are now met essentially by sand, one of the few media in which a child can release his imagination and leave his world different from the way he found it. The possibilities of further activity like this, with new construction items like large-scale Tinker Toys, or new materials like plastics, are only beginning.

For the utmost involvement and safety of the child, supervision is essential. The good "play leader" needs great quantities of materials, enterprise, and patience. His job is to encourage the child to become involved in his own environment—encourage him to experiment with construction and destruction —without subjecting him to excessive direction or discipline.

Ultimately, it should be possible to bring materials to a playground in carload lots. A child should be able to take part of the playground home with him, or bring part of it from home. The playground is no longer an immutable place.

Ultimately, in the playground of the future, the designer will build only the superstructure; the child will create the playground. At this point we are exploring parts of a permanent facility that a child could manipulate himself. One possibility is a giant abacus—perhaps with different colors on its two sides—a brilliant play piece to appeal to the child's delight in color, movement, learning. Another experimental design has adjustable rods with which a child can create changing spatial relationships, making new ladders and openings that he then uses for swinging and climbing. A continuing experiment is the addition by the child of colored panels, or works of art, to the more athletic play pieces, or the addition of water elements or bridges. Another play item is a series of large alphabet blocks up to three or four feet high set into a floor track; again, the child not only constructs his play environment but learns from it, spelling out words or learning arithmetic on the brilliantly colored blocks. The dual purpose of all of these is a direct involvement by the child in his environment, and an interplay among all aspects of that environment—visual, social, intellectual, and physical.

Eventually, the playground will see more of the formal learning experiences incorporated into it for a rich environment of discovery. Play equipment will have mirrors, magnifying glass, blackboards, combinations of colors and textures, equipment for hydraulic or mechanical experiments, pulley systems, and so on. The playground designer will be collaborating with the artist and the educator to create a world where learning and play are merged. As he "plays," the child will learn the wholeness of life instead of its fragmentation, and involvement instead of passivity. Play may not be the only—or even primary —salvation of the educational system that is now under such stress, but it could go a long way toward making learning an entirely new experience. It is possible that with new educational techniques, a child could be taught and not know he's being taught. Learning could *be* play.

This is all an experiment. If we commit ourselves to it, we can create an exciting environment for children and exciting possibilities for their development. As we learn more about child development, and see what involves a child, our ideas about play facilities will undoubtedly change, and will—in due course—look primitive in years to come.

Sliding—The standard manufactured slide is a poor accommodation for this natural activity. It is dangerous—the child can easily fall 8 to 10 feet incurring a major injury. The steps are standard for all slides, allowing a small child to use any slide and possibly overextend himself. The slide is awkward—shins may be cracked on the steel steps or at the top; balance is threatened in changing from standing to sitting. The slide is restrictive—it may be used by only one child at a time and only in the prescribed way. It denies interaction with others and offers no alternatives.

Imitate nature; extrapolate from the natural form; create a form that provides the option to slide, climb, traverse, or perch.

Motion is experience, excitement, and stimulation. Extend the physical capabilities of a child and you've made contact—he is involved. Make it meaningful, safe, and challenging and he learns.

Adventure at the end of a piece of rope.

Medieval torture contraptions—What is the toll in eyes extracted or in brain damage by these lethal instruments of recreation?

Swinging is safe; the swing is unsafe. The problem is in the design, not in the activity. A child hit by a tire suffers negligible damage, more to the psyche than to the body. Children become active participants in the direction to swing (360°), in the number that can swing, and in the speed. Groups interact, and games spring up among swingers. The new form of the design leads to multifaceted activities. Dollars buy play value in this geodesic dome; whereas, traditional superstructures take most of the money and give nothing in return but support.

The lure of motion—A child will seek any motion, like sliding or swinging. Extension of the child's physical capabilities gives him more in return than the small action he initiates— he challenges gravity by rolling, springing; he is bigger when he is higher; he is faster when he discovers the wheel.

Translation of the natural to the man-made.

Climb—to observe ; to dominate ; to hide ; to play explorers, mountain climbers, pilots, etc.

Jumping is as old as the desire to fly —
a test of the body against height.
Jumping itself is easy ; landing can be
hard.

Balancing is a skill in which the challenge develops a further understanding of gravity. The child is in constant competition with natural forces.

Natural materials must not be under-
stated when tamed for the urban
environment.

Water play is where the water is, regardless of what is legally permitted.

Barriers like signs are invitations to disregard. A child looks for challenge in his environment. A fence or a wall must be tested as to its adequacy before it can be honored.

Scale defines graduated levels of challenge and territory. Smaller children sit on the columns, older ones use them as a maze, and the oldest jump from one mountain top to the next. When design is scaled to only one group, it excludes others by intimation and activity.

Role-playing—Who am I? What can I be? What do I want to be? Every mask or object creates a new personality or situation. Children's dramas do not need a literal backdrop for their fantasies.

Literal design restricts a child's imagination, for he can bring to a playground, in his hand or in his mind, any fire engine. An object with only one use creates attitudes and experiences, with one dimension.

Nature and play—reflection, shadow, wind, sounds—are the interplays between nature and the child. The ecology of the city is rich in play and learning value.

Art and play if not spontaneous and unintentional must inevitably suffer. The artist's concern is the aesthetic; he comments on life through his art. Any compromise to an ancillary function diminishes the artist's first goal. Another dilemma of play art is realism; the literal definition of an animal finds its play value quickly exhausted. (This animal sculpture is at a large zoo and will not have to hold a child's interest for more than the day he visits.)

Expression—A child comes to understand art as a means of expression, both for himself and for others.

Construction play is the precursor of a new concept in playground design. The playground as we know it will ultimately become obsolete, and children will construct their own play environments. Construction play is a universal pastime for every age group; it is the unifying link between education and recreation.

The Teen-Ager

The teen-ager, no longer child and not yet adult, is betwixt and between in terms of recreation planning, too. No one has bothered to plan for the teen-ager and answer the needs that are special to this age. For that matter, no one has bothered to analyze what these needs are, for the purpose of planning, or has found in them any relationships on which the designer can build.

Unfortunately, teen-agers are not yet a politically urgent issue—at least not urgent enough to motivate politicians (or adults in general) to the necessary response. Teen-agers are a visible group, to be sure, but thus far without positive political power. Much of a city's troubles with crime, unemployment, and illegitimacy, however, are the product of teen-age disaffection and disorientation. Perhaps this negative political power—to frustrate and threaten the rest of society—will ultimately force attention to the true needs of the teen-ager. Exerting no effective political pressure on his own behalf, and engaging in a nondialogue with adults, he is left to find his own way.

This is a critical time between two worlds. The teen-ager is sometimes a child looking back to a time of dependence, sometimes an adult looking ahead to the responsibilities of maturity. Interchangeably, he uses a child's logic, then an adult's. And in between the two worlds, he has a world of his own, neither child's nor adult's—his own strong and influential subculture. Today's teen-ager has given the larger society a whole new style in music, dance, fashion, political protest; he is participating in, and creating, a whole new sexual revolution.

Teen-Age Drives and Values

What is he like? And what are his values?

He sees the adult world as a disillusioning place, with its major problems of poverty, racism, war. He sees automation as limiting his own job possibilities. He sees his education as a factory process, giving more of a credential as the end product than an experience of real value in itself. He wants to change this world before he has to inherit it. Being extremely verbal, he argues constantly with adults, antagonizing and alarming them; he repudiates their world and challenges them to a defense of what they themselves once thought indefensible.

As an individual, he is looking for his own identity, although he may dress ex- *91* actly like all his friends in order to attain his uniqueness. He is focused on his peers for approval and acceptance yet is highly susceptible to hero worship, admiring successful people in various fields (legitimate and otherwise). He is capable of organization—and eager for it—in anything from neighborhood teams to secret clubs. He is competitive. He looks for success and wants to have his successes recognized. He has tremendous amounts of intellectual, physical and sexual energy. He seeks adventure in a world that is increasingly urbanized and organized and that offers its adventures in increasingly stereotyped ways. He is fond of role playing, trying on various possibilities in new situations and with new people.

As a group, teen-agers want to be with one another—boys with girls, girls with boys—yet they want to pursue their separate interests, too, when these diverge. They want to be by themselves, away from the scrutiny of adults who may have only a faded memory of the painful sensitivities and strivings of adolescence.

Inadequate Facilities

Adults are perplexed by teen-agers; the teen-agers won't do what the adults want them to do but cannot be disciplined in the way they were as children. The easy way out, providing a few athletic facilities in the hope that they will keep teen-agers busy and "out of trouble," is no answer. The need is not for facilities that are simply diversional but for activities that are meaningful—and to teen-agers, not to us. We know that the existing facilities are not work-

ing, and small wonder when they are what the adult *wants* the teen-ager to have rather than what the teen-ager himself wants. Consistently the teen-ager disappoints the adult by an inability to communicate in terms of "reality." And the adult disappoints the teen-ager by an inability to comprehend. "They *have* a basketball court and a baseball field. What else do they want?" It should be obvious that the needs are more complex.

In fact, teen-agers have utterly inadequate facilities; the occasional basketball court or recreational hall is a one-dimensional experience. Teen-agers invade a facility designed specifically for another group, turning it into their exclusive "turf" not to harass others but because there is literally no other place for them. They hang around street corners because there is no other place. There can be no moral judgment against "hanging around on street corners" when it is seen as reflecting some instinct for territoriality, some need for a place where teen-agers can be with others like themselves, be noticed, and explore various relationships. Much of any social interaction is a kind of "hanging around"—against a backdrop of other activities that (more or less) provide the excuse for being together. The street corner is, however, deficient in providing other possibilities, or in directing the enormous potential of a teen-ager for his development in many directions.

A Special "Place"

Since there *is* this emerging period, with its particular style and expression, why not allow it full time and place to flower? Since teens *are* rebelling against the adult world, why not permit them the opportunity to create their own world as a comparison? They need an entirely new place, an enclave of their own where they can find other teen-agers—and, very often, *only* teen-agers.

This "place"—for the moment not more specifically defined—should be a complete social, athletic, recreational, educational world. Ideally, it should be the school itself in a new form, but this can happen only if the school is the true domain of the student, a place he thinks of as his own because he is at least partly responsible for its direction and tone. There are signs that this may come, but it is not here yet. For the present, unfortunately, the school does not belong to the students in any sense; instead, it subjects them to an authoritarianism we would cringe to read about in Dickens. Naturally resentful, the urban child is glad to get away from school at the end of a day or at the end of the legally required number of years.

When some teen-age boys in Bedford-Stuyvesant were recently asked what they wanted in the way of recreation facilities, they were alive with ideas. Basketball courts came first (perhaps because they thought this was the correct answer), then somewhere to dance and be with girls, somewhere to work and earn money, somewhere to eat. "How about using parts of the school for any of these?" they were asked. "Oh, no," they answered, in an immediate response that indicated the layers of resentment our educational system has built up. Anything that smacks of schooling is suspect, and it is sad to consider what this means in terms of the fragmentation of their lives, with the avenues forever closed. In their best sense, education and recreation are not separate. Budd Schulberg's creative writing workshop in Watts, where the teen-age boys met in a coffee shop, was the interplay of education and recreation in its highest form.

It is too bad not to be able to use school facilities built at great cost and vacant for large parts of the day and year, but nothing will be gained by pinning new forms to an image that is hopelessly alien. If the school can't function as the center of teen life, the alternative for the activities they need is a separate place.

New Possibilities

What elements would be in this separate place? A snack bar, a dance floor, a gym, a theater, a study hall? Perhaps all of these, or some, or others. The important thing is the way in which any of these is provided, permitting new possibilities to develop. Bleachers at the edge of a basketball court encourage girls to watch and allow the boys to show off in front of them. A snack bar run by the teen-agers is a social activity and might answer their wish to assume responsibility. But the teen-agers must be allowed to make the rules as well as the sodas. Will there be music or dancing or studying as an adjunct—or all three? Or other activities? Will there be workshops—for personal use, for classes, for selling things and earning money? Will there be meeting areas? Quiet areas? (Many teen-agers live in apartments too small to allow study at home.) Will there be shops for the clothes, records, sports equipment, and cosmetics that teen-agers want to buy? Any of these could be run by the teen-agers themselves. Will there be studios—for film making, music practicing, muscle building, dress designing, poster making, hair dressing, auto repairing, and so on?

New possibilities will be generated by new teen-agers and new times. It is essential that the place belong to the teen-agers and be built by them—not brick by brick, although that is an interesting proposition—but the programming must be developed by them, with adult advisers only as needed. The physical planning should be by professionals, but it should be such that the teen-agers are later free to manipulate their own environment to a considerable extent, free to run the place under their own initiative. They will want no part of it if it handed down to them, or handed over, complete.

Even though it is their own, however, it need not be totally apart from the rest of the community. Since role playing is an important part of the teen-age experience, theater may be a prominent activity, with occasional performances for the community at large. Since organized sports are important, intracity teams are a natural, with teen-agers gaining a sense of belonging to their neighborhood when it turns out to support them. Since hero worship is important, visits from outstanding figures are an obvious part of the program, not so much to teach full courses as on a more occasional schedule. Many children who are "troublemakers" at school have blossomed overnight from contact with an outside person or idea.

But these are all only possibilities. The checklist of a center's facilities is less important than the flexibility and freedom built into it. And the building itself is less important than the attitude prevailing in it; an old warehouse could be more than adequate, and the most lavish new building could be a dismal failure. The important aspects of the place are that it be the teen-ager's domain and that he bring it to whatever is meaningful to him. He is not a basketball player one day, a musician the next; he is first of all a teen-ager. The object of the place is not to mold the teen-ager into the patterns of *our* day but to provide the milieu through which he can create and adapt to the patterns of *his* day, which is yet to come. He must be allowed to experience and explore. The process of trial and error is essential to the learning process and the teen community provides the place for the process.

The teen-ager is not a fixed being. He is very much a becoming. And in these years, he can easily become lost—whole young generations are becoming lost to themselves and to the society. He will live in a new world partly of his own making. But he lives now in a world structured by adults. And the adult response to a teen-ager's experimenting, changing, rebelling, can make all the difference between successful growth and tragic waste. For the continued development of a vital society, can we afford to fix the teen-ager in a permanent role as dull automaton or resentful dropout?

The Adult

It is easiest to develop recreational facilities for the adult, because he is more self-sufficient and more mobile than any other age group. His environment is the whole city. But the adult—no less than any other age group—needs facilities that enrich his life on many levels and answer the complex needs of his particular life style. It is necessary to look beyond the adult counterpart of a set of swings or a solitary basketball court. These are not to the point. The adult requires an interplay of facilities —for himself alone, for himself and friends, for himself and his spouse, for himself and his children.

There are many kinds of adults in the city—of varied age, marital status, and income. Throughout this discussion our focus is on those of lower and middle income, who cannot afford to hire a plane, go on a cruise, or join an expensive country club. The fortunate few can take care of themselves, but the city must offer high-quality, low-cost recreation close to home for all its residents.

The urban adult, then, can be defined essentially by his age and family status. He (or she) may be young and unattached, a migrant to the city from out of town—perhaps transient, perhaps planning to live permanently in the city. He seeks places in the city (in some cases bars, in other cases more structured social clubs) where he can meet a new friend or a potential mate. But the city is hostile, and, having few places for those without roots, it breeds loneliness. Its lack of hospitality is more easily seen by newcomers, but all city dwellers experience it.

Or the adult is the family man, his recreational needs inextricably tied up with his children, wife, parents, and other adults. He wants to spend time with various members of his family on weekends (and in the evenings), but he doesn't want to cut himself off from his friends. He needs places for active team sports and special interests on his own, he needs local facilities for short periods of time with his family, and he needs larger (necessarily more distant) facilities for full-day excursions.

Or the adult is the shopper, single or married, for whom shopping (and window-shopping) are a major recreation—a pastime and necessity of excitement. Unfortunately, it is often a harassing experience, isolated from any other activity that could contribute real recreational value. The need is for a shopping environment with an interplay of shopping and entertainment;

the recreation is in the shopping, the dining, the commercial entertainment and also in being where the crowds are.

And the adult of any age and sex is a part of the life of the city, a participant in its *public* events, wanting to be in closer contact with them than at the receiving end of a solitary TV tube. The adult is also a spectator at *commercial* events (movies, sports, theater, excursions, exhibits), finding that the environment surrounding these events does not contribute to the experience but instead detracts from it. Other intrusions on his enjoyment are the demeaning journey getting there, and long lines and overcrowded facilities once he has arrived. The adult pays for much of his entertainment in money; unhappily, he also pays for it in aggravation.

The adult is many people. Only by looking at the specific needs of each of these types of urban dweller can the city begin to provide the recreational facilities that are appropriate.

Adults with Children

The young family needs recreation close to home, within the convenient radius that makes for easy toddling or wheeling distance for small children. But the family operates on various levels; members of the family will want to do some things as individuals, some things as a family. The facility should be addressed to the different age groups in the family as well as to the family as a whole.

The neighborhood facility will be a mixture of playground (for all age groups), gym, and community center. It should include 1) eating places of

some sort, as modest as a vendor or as sophisticated as a cafe; 2) areas where the parents can watch their children at play (although some may not want to; customs vary with different groups); 3) studios where the family can do some activities together, following the lead of the parent-child painting classes at the Museum of Modern Art in New York; 4) facilities for group games, like father-and-son races; 5) meeting places for the parents without their children —for hobbies, cards, dances. (Many of the facilities in a neighborhood center will also be attractive to the single adult, but the parent who has been away from his children all day or all week will especially appreciate the choice of as much or as little recreational contact with his children as he wants.)

The community will grow with these resources even when it is not aware of

the potentialities at the outset. At Riis Houses, when we designed an amphitheater into a neighborhood that had not shown a demand for one, we hedged our bets somewhat, letting it double as a spray pool. But the amphitheater is now widely used as a public podium— by teen-agers, by protest groups, by local churches, by the Parks Department, in short, by amateurs and professionals from inside the community and out.

City-Wide Facilities

The logical extension of the neighborhood facility is the *city-wide* facility with a similar interplay of activities. Here the young family can make an all-day excursion to a zoo or museum, a trip prompted by the children's interests but with enough further attraction to suit the adults, and satisfy the variety of reasons for which people go to a zoo or museum. This does not suggest that adults and children will want to go their separate ways in a large resource like a museum or aquarium, but it does suggest that we should begin to develop an orientation toward more than a single activity, more than a single age group. The adult will want exhibits and informational programs of his own while the child is preoccupied, and will want eating places of his own while the child is impatient for further explorations.

The major parks, too, should offer enough activity and complexity for an all-day family outing with a sequence of activities to be sampled, lingered over, or bypassed. The place should be different for the family each time they visit it; they should be able to see different things in it each time. Travel time for the all-day excursion may be long, and the family should not feel it has exhausted the possibilities of a place in only two or three hours. Variety in a full day's recreation is the spice of real re-creation.

During the day, there should be many recreational activities—swimming, theater, nature study, baseball, dining (even an opportunity to buy and prepare one's own picnic, with hot dogs and other raw materials for sale, barbecue grills for rent). If there is enough interplay among these activities, the individual members of a family can enjoy themselves without necessarily doing everything together. The adults can have a cool drink on a terrace overlooking the play area, and they and their children will be in as much contact with each other as each wants.

At night these parks should be alive with activity instead of dead (and deadly) as they now are. Life-giving activities will include light projections (from the traditional movies to the newest light pieces and the greatest light show man has ever devised—fireworks); large-screen TV; spectator sports; participation games and contests; drama of all kinds, rehearsed or improvised; music and dancing (we have taken the romance out of our parks because of our mania about maintenance)—and so on. The few examples of programmed evening activity in New York City— like Shakespeare-in-the-Park or the Philharmonic or the appearance of popular performers—have been so thoroughly enjoyed that it is surprising not to see every city follow suit.

The large park is also one of the few *97*

outdoor urban places where people gather as members of a community. Here is the place—night or day—for political rallies, discussions of civic questions, and appearances by public personalities.

One-Dimensional Places

Jones Beach is a classic example of the one-dimensional situation, with everyone arriving together before noon and departing together before sundown. The harassing journey on overloaded highways would be immediately eased if there were a diversity of activities at the beach, to draw people when there is no sun and keep them after the sun goes down. Variety would make the day a richer one, in addition to spacing out the cars that now leave the parking lots in long, bumpered strings. The solution to a mechanical problem often has added benefits as by-products.

But the real problem of urban recreation for the family is not to be solved at a Jones Beach. The answer lies closer to home. It is a paradox that while these traffic jams worsen each year, our cities still have miles of waterfront close to the urban centers. If these waterfronts were not almost universally polluted (and one Midwest river is so badly polluted that it is considered a fire hazard!), thousands of families could find recreation near home. Reclamation of these beaches and waterfronts is an absolute necessity. And the need is for parks that do not simply line the water but punctuate the city with their recreational activity. The object is not to make the city look green from the river, but to make the river look good to the residents and make the city alive again to its core.

The Single Adult

The adult without a family has his own special needs—primarily a place where he can go to meet new friends or be with familiar ones. Most of his recreation time is now spent at commercial places, attending movies and sports events, dancing, eating and drinking (many bars develop their character as places where particular groups of singles hang out).

Since loneliness *is* the overwhelming problem of a large group of city people, the city must try to answer it. Open spaces should foster, or at least not inhibit, social interplay among this group. Rich programming—music, dancing, and other special activities—should be designed to appeal to the young and more mature adult. The possibilities are not limited to the major parks and plazas; many smaller spaces could support and be improved by special programs and facilities. A mobile food vendor or a food kiosk near home would be welcomed by many single adults; these facilities need not have the repellent quality of our standard quick-lunch places—no nonsense and no fun—but could be modeled after the relaxed civility of the European sidewalk cafe, or the holiday flavor of a booth at a fair.

A dining facility need not be costly to the city. Bethesda Fountain in Central Park is a case in point. With a foundation grant and a franchise to a major restaurant group, Thomas Hoving, then Parks Commissioner, turned this underutilized area into a meeting place whose success can be measured by its long waiting lines. Teen-agers and adults stand in line up to an hour to be able to look out over a lake while they eat. The spot offers an interplay of activities— dining (at two price levels), boating, guitar playing, fountain watching, even swimming (some children use the fountain as the local pool)! It is exciting socially, in a most contemporary way, and is magnificently romantic in the setting created by Frederick Law Olmsted. Its operation provides continuing income to the city, paying for maintenance here and elsewhere. And this boon didn't cost the city a penny! (Another of Hoving's moneyless moves concerned bicycle routes. After no little protest he managed to have all roads in Central Park closed to cars on Saturdays and Sundays, so that now, without

any outlay of money, the city has a recreational resource of incalculable pleasure to adults, children, families. This is a case in point that recreation is not always a function of money but many times a function of imagination.

Excitement in Shopping

For the woman of any age, shopping is not only a necessity but a recreation; buying a new hat or a new washing machine is fun. The shopping itself is involving, with its attention-getting displays, and interplay between people who may not even be in overt communication with one another. Unfortunately, this stimulation is usually restricted to the experience of shopping itself—either the window-shopping or the actual shopping; there is little in the immediately surrounding public environment that makes the most of the mood or enlarges upon it. Rockefeller Center is one of the rare examples of an exciting backdrop to shopping, where restaurants, floral displays, ice skating, flags (not even "art" but just ordinary national flags), add their magnetism to the shopping. Rockefeller Plaza is alive with people. In the summer there are diners outdoors, banners waving in the wind, people moving through the narrow streets, and pouring into the plaza. In the winter, ice skating and Christmas displays are the lure. The area is one of tension and release, activity and movement, tall buildings in relation to low ones. There seem always to be more people watching than doing; for every skater there are probably ten or fifteen observers, and for every diner, three or four people licking their chops.

Any major shopping area should have this variety—indoor and outdoor dining, displays, band concerts, parades, spectacles, happenings, fashion shows, sculpture, pennants, color, sound—the varied components to be structured by a public body but operated privately. As time progresses, these programs will extend well beyond our present imagination. The magnetism of the downtown shopping area could be so powerful that people from all parts of the city and region would be drawn inward, and the downtown would extend a constant invition to participate in the public and commercial life of the times. In ancient days the civic spaces were intimately tied up with the shopping areas; we have only to look back in history to see where to go in the future.

Lessons from the Suburbs

Not only in variety of activities but also in variety of spaces (and the two are related) are urban shopping areas missing an opportunity. Most downtown shopping areas are linear, all movement; there is no sense of going there just to *be* there. The suburban shopping center, on the other hand, although surrounded by an abhorrent sea of cars, has developed an interior mall that is a significant place, a place lacking in the city. The mall is often the suburb's only large contained space, and because of its uniqueness, it finds a place in the life of the community—for proms, graduations, exhibitions (cars, sailboats, hobbies, and so on)—that no other space can fulfill.

Now, with the changing land costs in suburbia, the shopping centers are be-ginning to deck over their parking, and it is conceivable that these centers will become the cores of newly emerging urban areas. Offices want to locate here, as do churches and social services. Rapid transit interchanges will most logically be here. It is true that much of the esthetics and planning of the suburban shopping center is at the meanest level of public and commercial taste, but there is a vitality in the place that over-rides the details. Unless we see what makes it attractive, however, the suburban shopping center will sap the strength of the downtown center, not only in economic terms but also socially. In the sincerest form of flattery, downtown should seek to emulate this kind of civic and recreational place, a place for celebration, a place that does not fragment the person into his separate functions but enriches any one of his activities by putting it in the context of his other needs.

A city may have more than one shopping area, but each of these "shopping areas" should have more than the one activity of shopping in it. And the types of spaces (large plazas, narrow alleys, promenades, bridges, multilevel terraces, etc.) should be geared to the various types of activities. It will be impossible—and unnecessary, in any case—to anticipate all desired activities since some will arise spontaneously out of the needs of future times; however, a variety of spaces will permit a considerable amount of latitude in their use.

Shopping areas can be stimulating places even on Sunday when stores are closed; thousands of people have entered Montreal's underground concourse at

Place Ville Marie on a Sunday just for window-shopping and to watch the other people who are window-shopping (and watching them!). Even in bad weather, a shopping area has its magnetism; eventually the climate of many public places will be completely controlled, by retractable roofs, geodesic domes, and the like.

For mood or ambience, we can learn much from the suburban shopping center. The notion of sitting in tropical splendor in the shopping mall is a genuine and delightful fantasy, even though the details may strike us as tawdry. We can also learn from television, on which the commercials are often more imaginative than the programs sandwiched between them. There is a place for garishness and humor in our urban scene, and the shopping area is such a place.

This does not suggest that cities become corny or grotesque, but it does suggest that they loosen up.

The average adult will find that his recreation area is downtown—the theaters, movie houses, restaurants, cabarets of the big city. And in the biggest city of them all, it is a special entertainment just *being* in Times Square. Certain human needs are superbly met in this confluence of first-run films, all-night movie houses, tourist-and-bargain shops, pornographica purveyors, vibrant advertising displays. The puritanical hope of "cleaning out the mess" or "uprooting the unsavory elements" in Times Square (and in its counterparts in every large urban area) should be resisted. Progress in recreation will not be measured in terms of purity.

Low-Density Activities

More strenuous forms of recreation pose a different problem in the city; many athletic pastimes—tennis, baseball, track, golf, horseback riding—are low-density activities that require a great deal of precious urban land to serve very few participants. Potential space for some of these activities—primarily the racquet sports—is on the rooftops, now inefficiently used. The space required for a tennis court, for instance, is not vast and can easily be accommodated on an expanse of roof. Swimming pools should also be off the ground (thus also avoiding the visual scar during winter shutdown). Roofs hold many recreational possibilities as parks-in-the-sky that we have not yet probed; we have not even taken advantage of them for views.

Activities that require linkages with other activities must necessarily remain at or near ground level. And until the ground is sufficiently developed to have a natural vitality, recreation should not utilize the roofs. (In fact, to avoid seriously diluting urban cohesiveness on ground level, the open-space standards of the National Recreation Association should be reassessed.) Eventually, roofs can become another path system in the city, creating a rich multilevel intricacy for the city. Our elevators today enable us to live on many levels, but the city is not yet multilevel. With higher densities and new urban forms, recreational facilities, too, will be multilevel and vertical.

Transportation as Fun

Most recreational activities for the adult are not within walking distance of his home, and urban transportation can all but destroy the pleasure that is the purpose of the trip. Subways generally are so disagreeable that people turn off from everything outside themselves. But the subways could come alive—with shopping or entertainment facilities like discothèques and movie theaters. With changing displays and events, traveling the same route every day could be a new experience. Or the trip itself could have built-in variety, going from underground to above ground or from one differently designed station to the next. There should be a desire to take a subway ride because of the adventure of it. The minirail at Expo '67 was not just for transit but for the excitement of moving at different elevations, past different sights, and into different build-

ings along the route. The cars went under waterfalls, along shopping streets, into the domed U.S. pavilion. This variety could be developed in a "real" transportation system as well. Transportation is not only a matter of business, a way of getting to a job; it is also a way of getting to recreation, and it can be a form of recreation. The trip should be considered part of the total recreational experience.

Keeping the Senses Alive

Essentially, the problem of recreation for the adult returns to that of linkage. People are not fragmented; they are (or can be) whole personalities. But because of the way the environment now stimulates us (or abrades us), we learn as we grow older to shut off more and more of our senses—to respond selec-

tively and narrowly. The urban adult learns to turn off, not to experience life; he learns this from the inhumanity of the transportation system, from the hurrying he encounters in almost every restaurant, and from the many aspects of the city that are too small, too crowded, too noxious to let him breathe free. Faced with the hostility of the city, the adult responds with the blank stare, the self-hypnotic trance. With enough blows to the senses, he becomes insensate.

If the problem with children is to stimulate them, with adults it is to keep them aware. The commercial world understands this, calling us to attention with large signs, with unusual ads and displays, and with happenings.

The happening is not a gimmick but an important device to involve people

more directly in the life around them. Ken Dewey, the environmental artist, recently scored a series of happenings in Stockholm. (The artist traditionally is a communicator; the environmental artist does the same thing—by extrapolating from the existing environment, he sensitizes us to it and demands our involvement in it.) In one of Dewey's programs, a bass fiddler got off a bus and suddenly began to play in the middle of a square. Simultaneously a ballerina arrived, by taxi, and joined him in a dance. When they had finished, they left—in the same way. People were stunned. For days afterward, people looked at the simplest occurrences around them, asking, "Is *that* a happening?" The unusual had caused them to look far more closely at their environment. They were alert and sensitive to it, in ways that they had never been before.

We may not want to use the happening directly, but its concept is instructive. Depending on its qualities, the environment can cause people to close themselves off, in defense, or open themselves up to its richness and to one another. The urban adult, whose recreational environment is the whole city, needs a city that catalyzes social interplay, that stimulates and satisfies him, that is dynamic and constantly providing the possibility of re-creation.

Energy and time, the teen-ager's great untapped resources, are denied any meaningful outlet. Sports become the only permissible outlet, and sports are just one-dimensional, while young people have many dimensions and potentialities.

Disorientation is the current malaise of the teen-ager. With nothing to do and nowhere to go, the teen-ager lives through a time of disorientation, restlessness, and confrontation.

Turf is identification and security. Since society makes no special provision for the teen-ager, we witness constant conflicts over turf. Teen-agers need a special place somewhat separate from the mainstream of society, but not excluded from it.

Style is a cultural by-product of teen-age freedom and experimentation. Concepts and form are tested on each other. They have already seen their ideas in music and dress bring a revolution to society at large.

Transition is the process and maturity is the goal. Faced with changes he needs to understand—responsibilities and commitments to himself and others—he is thrust into times that are both frightening and exciting.

Subculture, a culture within a culture, where new styles, moralities, concepts, and methods are pitted against old institutions and tradition. They have embarked on a search for new human relationships and rational values. Theirs is a quest for relevancy, for constructive human contact. Their festivals and celebrations are for the purpose of being together. Teen-agers don't have the answers, but they do have the questions; their impact is not to be denied.

Adult recreation describes a three-dimensional pattern having physical, social, and cultural components. There is not a clear line between commercial and public sectors of adult recreation. Jogging, dining, movies, theater, education, museum galleries, etc. are the matrices of adult recreation. Future parks may show a marriage of the public and private sectors to provide for adult needs.

History may provide new recreational
experiences drawn from tradition.
Bicycling was once the cherished
pastime of pre-automotive adults.

Adaption and adoption of historical precedents can restore a scale of living now forgotten. The recreational life of the 1880s—often richer than today's —is reinstated at the Bethesda Fountain's new restaurant which is nothing more than a restoration of former richness.

The Family with young children finds
that the recreation needs of the two
generations will often merge. The
family wants to be together in leisure
time, but in such a way that each person
is able to do what interests him.

Programming can exploit the dynamics between an existing physical resource and an imposed activity. The street becomes a museum; the playground becomes a gallery. Music by a local steel drum band provided the magnet, and the paintings provided the experience. This event completely transformed the playground into a place, a festival, a museum, and a gallery. Space is a resource that can provide many uses and forms.

Loneliness and apathy will be the diseases of tomorrow. A new form of recreation will contribute to the cure. Facilities, institutions, and events will bring people together for shared experience; education will be recreation. Understanding through a knowledge of oneself and others will provide the catalyst for physical and social relationships. Our resources must not continue to be wasted on standardized, desolate places for loners who sit together, searching for a means of contact.

The Elderly

Every age group is neglected in its recreational needs, but the elderly—less self-sufficient than others—can sustain the neglect least easily.

It is one of the disturbing paradoxes of modern times that we take great care to lengthen life but do little to give meaning to the added years. We spend almost unlimited money to keep people alive but almost nothing to make their lives worth the living. We have created a new elderly population but have done little to create a new life for them. This is particularly true in the city, where the environment is more hostile to the elderly than in times past.

The Need to Be Productive

The elderly are the product of a day now past, with its wholehearted espousal of the Protestant ethic: work is honored, leisure is not. For the elderly of today, work and diligence are still a primary good; dignity and self-sufficiency *through work* are still a paramount goal. Even in retirement, the older person is not ready for a life without work and remuneration. Unlike the nobility of the past, or the jet set of the present, the average elderly person cannot accept a life of leisure, even when he is told he has earned it. Future generations will undoubtedly become used to the ideas of early retirement and a guaranteed annual wage—it is not farfetched to anticipate an annual stipend *not* to work in the days of greater automation ahead—but today's elderly population is not so flexible.

This was most clearly seen when an activity program was proposed for a nursing home in Cleveland. Music gardens, waterfalls, chess tables, flower beds, art exhibits, sitting areas, and other idyllic features were suggested. The director of the home said, "These are all the right attitudes, in wanting to provide things to do, but all the wrong ideas. The real desire of our elderly is to work in our small factory, to be productive and earn a little money. Everything else might be very nice—in addition— but they want to be stimulated by their *own* activity."

The elderly must have a productive place in the society today—a functioning place in the physical, economic, and social sense. This place can be forged only out of the realistic evaluation of the new elderly—who they are and what they need. The old answers are not good enough anymore.

Loneliness and Dependence

Who are the elderly?

They are lonely, essentially, with a great desire to be in contact with others, since they live more vicariously than actively.

They are limited in mobility. They still have a certain self-sufficiency, but their physical and financial resources are likely to be already limited and growing more so.

They are dependent on one another. They find it most comfortable to live near one another, retreating into the easy relationships they have—relationships that are both more accepting of and more dependent on one another than earlier in their lives. Their dependence comes from the need for mutual aid, and for companionship, as they grow more alone and more subject to sudden illness. Their quick acceptance of one another is part of the transient quality of their society, with its sudden and frequent deaths, making it necessary to find new friends as old ones die and giving the elderly a broader tolerance of the human condition as life proceeds.

They want access to the world but want to retreat from noise and activity at their own discretion. It used to be argued that dwelling units for the elderly should be sprinkled throughout the community. Now, however, it is conceded that housing can better meet their needs (individually and as a group) if they live together in their own housing complex. At Pruitt-Igoe housing in St. Louis, where there are a few apartments for the elderly on each floor, much of the vacancy—which is very high—is attributable to the older person's not wanting to live among families

of three and four children. A similar project in St. Louis, where the elderly live separately, is 100 per cent occupied. It is a finely drawn line; the elderly do not want to be shut off from the rest of society, but they *do* want to be able to pull back and live at their own pace.

They want to feel useful and productive. There is at present no route to full membership in this society other than money received for work performed. After forty and fifty years of work, the elderly have a desire to continue using their experience and expertise in productive ways, and a need to feel useful that can be satisfied only by work and compensation.

An Untapped Reservoir

What, then, is recreation for people with these needs? Paradoxically, a good part

of their recreation will be work, in a variety of forms. Recognizing this fact, we can manage to keep the elderly a part of society in ways beneficial both to themselves and to the population as a whole. Not recognizing it, we will in effect be suggesting that they go out and die when they feel "useless," much as the Eskimo culture does. Struggling in an economy with limited food, the Eskimo goes off to die when he is no longer productive; no one tells him when to go, and no one stops him. We do almost the same thing in our own society when we condemn the elderly to the indignity of obsolescence; we ask "only" for spiritual death, not physical death, but it is nevertheless a serious crime against a growing number of people.

If the problem of the elderly is the need to feel productive and useful, the

solution lies in exploring meaningful ways to utilize their talents and resources. One of the chief resources of the elderly is *time,* which they can offer in periods of short duration. The elderly also have *skills* from four or five decades of work. They have *patience.* They have *eyes,* and a physical presence that goes far in policing areas and in providing unofficial surveillance for the community.

These resources mesh with the needs of the society. In recreation-oriented work alone, there are many marginal jobs not now being performed—operation of kiosks, key shops, greenhouses, food-vending stands, and the many other park services that are desirable but not usually considered essential, programmed but not usually provided —because of the high cost of labor. Their absence deprives us of amenity and convenience (one thinks of the chair rental concessions in London parks) and romance (one imagines the hurdy-gurdy or other musicians throughout the city). The elderly could well fit into many such part-time jobs. Facilities that are beyond limited municipal budgets could be carried out on a continuing basis without public money (after the initial outlay for programming). Private companies could provide the equipment, lease the franchises, and keep the facilities maintained with part of the earnings.

Training and teaching programs are other areas of part-time potentiality for the elderly. We have only recently come to understand the tremendous impact on the student of a one-to-one ratio between student and teacher. The demand is certainly great—another case of the needs of the society not fully met and a group in the society not fully utilized.

What could the elderly teach? Carpentry, electrical work, mechanical trades, cooking, writing, painting, crafts, clerical skills, language, music, photography, and so on. It is paradoxical that an older person's craft may be recreation for the youngster—or the older person may, on the other hand, be providing the serious training that leads to an occupation for the youngster.

At the younger age levels there is a need for reading, storytelling, companionship, and the interest in a child that urges him to learn. Programs for preschool enrichment require many persons—young and old—to bring the outside world to children who have led insulated lives.

These are not just programs to keep older people busy but programs to put a lifetime of skills to use. They are not just make-work but programs to apply talents built up over decades. They are also programs to provide needed instruction to young people, and to keep the elderly an active part of the society. Underlying it all is the symbiotic relationship between old people who are lonely and young people who need special attention and education.

Places for Congregating

By a similar logic, if one of the major problems of the elderly is loneliness, the answer is to create places that induce them to come together and socialize. The answer will grow out of examining the places where they now congregate, see-ing what elements make up their experiences, and abstracting from this whatever ideas are instructive.

Major points of social contact today are the cafeterias where the elderly can sit for long periods of time undisturbed by hustling waiters, where there is no pressure to vacate the tables, no pressure to buy more food. Here they find their own milieu, occupying the cafeteria as if it were a social club. The designer can easily see the meaningful aspects of this experience—inexpensive food, plenty of people to watch, the absence of pressure to move on, the sitting areas protected from the weather. It simply remains for the designer to provide these in a humane way in a new situation. Hundreds of parks and other places throughout a city could have self-service cafeterias. Some of these, in

fact, could be run by the elderly themselves, with their time and managerial talents to spare.

Other congregating places are the benches on traffic islands; Upper Broadway is the prime example. What a contradiction: even the ghastly fumes of a major traffic street do not keep this from being one of the most popular places for sitting. And why? Because of the need to observe the passing activity without being directly in its path. Watching—from windows, sidewalks, door stoops—is a universal pastime for the elderly. People are the landscape of the city and people-watching is one of the chief activities of the older person. In their passive way, the elderly sustain their own life by relating to the activity that goes on about them.

It is time for the designer to recog-

nize these as facts of life and design for them. The elderly don't really want to be adrift in seas of carbon monoxide, but they *do* want to see other people, to look at what interests them instead of being isolated from the life of the city. Their need to be among people forces them into this malevolent environment. The components of the existing pastime —observing people—need to be restructured to take place in more cordial and comfortable surroundings. Sitting areas need to be closely integrated with the passing throng but out of the path of exhaust fumes and sidewalk traffic. There is an instructive lesson to be learned from the Riis project, where the elderly were provided with a place of their own, carefully cloistered from the more boisterous people who would also be using the large plaza. The elderly, however, wanted none of this seclusion and went out on the sidewalk again where they could be participants —however passively—in the drama of life. (The walled-off area has since been taken over by teen-agers, who very much want a place of their own.)

The city offers many other forms of potential recreation for the elderly. Travel in the city is itself a form of recreation—not travel *to* recreation but travel *for* recreation. Many journeys taken as a matter of course by the busy person can be a stimulating enjoyment for the less active person. Since observing the life of the city and its people is a delight to the older person with time to spend, moving through the city without major exertion should be high on the list of potential recreations. If a traffic island on Broadway gives the satisfaction of watching life and movement, how rich the simplest bus ride could be. Off-peak hours offer an opportunity for reduced fares, encouraging travel by the elderly. Special river excursions during weekdays offer another opportunity; these are empty seats otherwise. The double-decker bus should not have been retired from Fifth Avenue in New York, no matter how compelling the practical considerations were at the time. With the demise of that bus, another bit of romance departed from the city and another of the most inexpensive recreational facilities for young and old alike was lost.

Meaningful Activities

Although their energies are limited, the elderly are still interested in physical activity. Bocce and shuffleboard are possibilities, but not in great demand. The sedentary games—chess and checkers, cards, dominoes—have more appeal; a chess area in Manhattan's Central Park, for instance, draws its attendance almost literally from the elderly population of New York's five boroughs. There is no question that the elderly like to play cards, checkers, and the like, but here again we must look more closely at the attraction of a checkers table: it draws people together who only incidentally will then play this game with each other; they go there primarily in order to be together. Providing an isolated checkers table is thus no solution; any such facility must be linked with other facilities—other attractions—in order to serve the overriding function of providing a place where elderly people will find others like themselves.

Basically, then, the need is for areas that provide social encounters while also providing a place to play a particular game. Linking the place and activity together means that each reinforces the other, with the combination providing an experience of real meaning.

We must look closely at the new lives of a new elderly population. Their needs won't be solved by simple beautification or an odd facility here or there, but only by what comes out of a rigorous commitment to understanding the nature of the group. In many cases their recreational needs will be the antithesis of what we think. Our purpose is to provide activities that *they* consider meaningful, not that *we* consider meaningful, and jobs that are important in themselves and not make-work.

New recreational facilities are in order. Through intuition and common sense, through experimentation and evaluation of what they have and what we proceed to provide, we have a basis for beginning to meet their needs. As we look around at what is now offered the elderly in terms of recreation—the dismal and patronizing centers for "senior citizens," the facilities lacking even minimal appropriateness and grace —it is as if we have told our elderly to drop out of society and out of our sight. With more and more older people present in the population, this neglect is neither fair to them nor worthy of the rest of us. The point that may give greatest impetus for reconsidering the plight of the elderly, however, is the sobering thought that it's only a matter of time before we are *all* "golden-aged."

Improvisation can transform a chain into a chair or a bench. Observation is a good teacher for designers, for many needs are apparent through use and activities.

Understanding the real needs. The lure of the traffic island is its centrality, its ringside seat on life. The park benches are empty because nothing is happening there. The designer's job is to answer the real needs—in this case, to provide for the traffic island's excitement and sense of community while eliminating its deleterious fumes and noise.

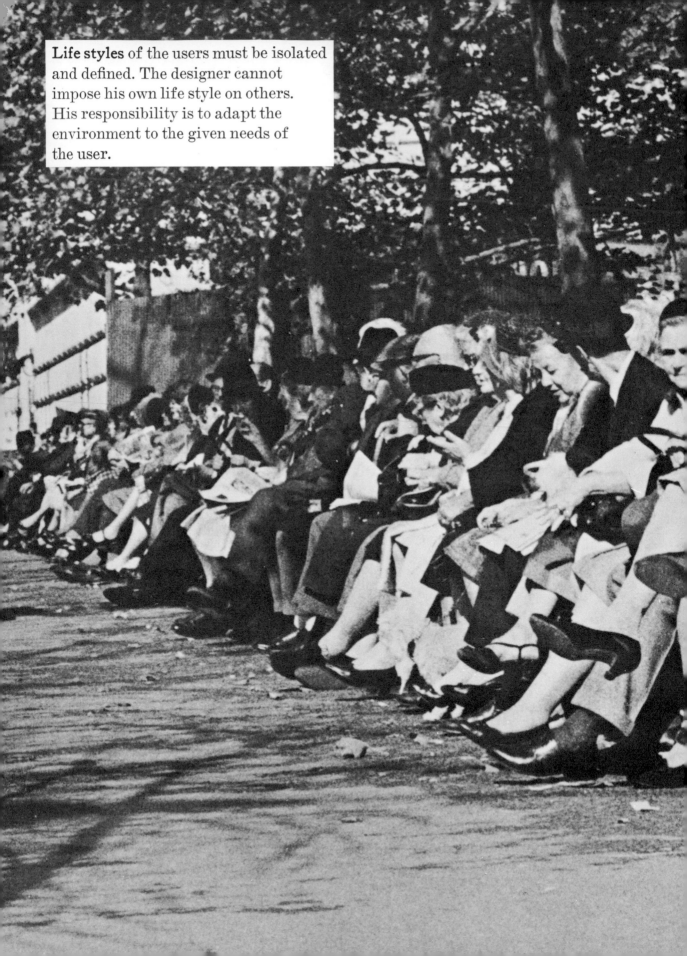

Life styles of the users must be isolated and defined. The designer cannot impose his own life style on others. His responsibility is to adapt the environment to the given needs of the user.

Passive and active roles are part of any recreational experience. If this game were isolated, away from the main street, few would come to play or watch. The designer needs to know the full meaning of the experience to both its active and its passive participants.

Companionship is a major need for the elderly. They come from all over New York City to this chess corner in Central Park, to play and to watch, to be together knowing that this is where their action is.

Interplay is the new pattern. Both young and old gain from interaction. A recognition of interplay among people, places, facilities, and institutions is essential to a meaningful approach to recreation. We waste our resources through fragmentation.

The smallest vest pocket park in the world.

Vest Pocket Parks

Although a recent development, the vest pocket park is already a legend, burdened with magical attributes. And although it is true that the vest pocket park can have extraordinary effect for its size (like many mythical creations), we should look closely at what it is—and what it is not—in order to use it best in the real world.

Growing out of the "neighborhood commons" work by Karl Linn in Washington and Philadelphia during the 1950s, the neighborhood vest pocket park is now as much an economic and political tool as a physical one. Physically, it is simply the use of leftover land available in dense residential areas, using these vacant lots for the two age groups that have least mobility in the community—the very young (up to the age where they can cross streets alone) and the very old.

But in the process the vest pocket park can do several things of primary importance—mobilize a community and give it a sense of itself as an active participant in its own future; establish the techniques and structure by which the community can move on to make demands and decisions in larger projects; bring jobs and money, dignity and pride, into areas where they have been minimal; train residents in practical skills to give them entry into the larger society.

Initiating a Project

A vest pocket park can come into being in various ways. The community can initiate the process, going directly to a governmental agency (parks or recreation department). In one city, Philadelphia, a special fund for vest pocket parks is available in the municipal budget. Or the community can go to private sources. Foundations have been responsive (one of the Bedford-Stuyvesant parks in Brooklyn received aid from the Rockefeller Brothers Fund), as have large commercial groups (another of the parks in Bedford-Stuyvesant was sponsored by a local department store that saw its responsibility—and self-interest—in aiding the community).

In the process of getting the vest pocket park, the community learns how to express its demands to government and institutions. The experience becomes a testing ground for the residents, from which they can move on to larger ventures—perhaps sponsorship of housing. The vest pocket park is small enough to provide an immediate and comprehensible goal, large enough to have all the ingredients of any planning project.

What if the community is, as yet, unorganized and inarticulate? One of the strongest myths today is that unless a community is articulate enough to ask for a vest pocket park, it shouldn't have one. But if the community is at the edge of subsistence, the pressures on individuals may be so great that the community *as a community* is not articulate. The children in this kind of neighborhood need a recreation facility no less (and perhaps more) than those in a more vocal community. In the short run, a designer may find it easier to work with a more motivated and expressive group, which may be more responsive in the preliminary stages of design; in the long run, however, these qualities of organization and expression can be developed precisely through the creation of the park.

The Community's Participation

We have learned, at long last, that a community can't be *given* facilities, dumped into an empty lot like so much sand being delivered to a sandbox. But a new myth has replaced the old. It is now said that the community should design its own facilities. This is either an oversimplification or an error, depending on how the word "design" is meant. Let's examine the argument.

The relationship between designer and community is a subtle one. The designer has much to learn from the community—who its people are, what their needs are. He may not understand an unfamiliar family structure, a different population profile, a high proportion of low-skilled workers. The people in the community must communicate with the designer. They must show him what they are like; they can prepare inventories and canvass opinions for him, and they will obviously influence him. But they do not design. A community does not have the special training to translate its needs into three-dimensional design. It cannot advance itself in this way, although it clearly can advance the designer in *his* awareness.

There are many examples of successful communication and its mutual benefit. In Bedford-Stuyvesant, for instance, the community raised the problem of security, and the designer suggested lighting in lieu of fencing (lighting was chosen); also in Bedford-Stuyvesant, the community raised the question of control, to keep children from running into the street, and the designer depressed the park several steps to avoid fencing it off as a thing apart. This communication process shouldn't be limited to vest pocket parks, obviously, but should be operative whenever designers are working directly with the real client—the community—and not with far-off management.

The mechanism is not an easy one. A large open meeting is not the answer, because of its easy leap into bedlam, because one or two vociferous persons can disrupt a large group and prevent reasonable decision making, or because of its slow fall into mediocrity, where the end product resembles a little of everything but lacks its own identity. A satisfactory technique, employed by the

148

architect I. M. Pei in Bedford-Stuyvesant in the superblock project, was to set up a design committee from the community to work with the designers. In this case, the committee was party to all decisions and was continually going back and forth to the larger community (which possibly found the ideas easier to accept coming from their own representatives).

Paternalistic Attitudes

But in the end it is the designer who designs, to the problems as he sees them. The poor designer rarely can understand the problems for which he is designing.

The poor designer, too, is one who doesn't advance the community beyond its present situation. An amphitheater, for instance, needn't direct a commu-

nity into any specified behavior that is not authentically its own. An amphitheater is simply a resource that can reflect the feeling of the community in the ways in which it is programmed.

Under our usual paternalism, any new and different facility seems to convey to the bestower the right to say, "I've given you something, now use it well and change your ways." It doesn't work this way. Years of patience may go by before a facility is used in any way approaching what the designer had in mind. It may never be, and perhaps rightly so, in some cases.

The designer is only providing resources that allow growth—inducing it if possible, but essentially just allowing it. There is no guarantee that growth will occur, just as plants that are watered only do not all flourish; some require more to grow. We should dispel the myth that assumes a direct response from every action. And we should dispense with the patronizing attitude that says, "Unless you appreciate my gift, *in my terms,* you don't deserve it."

Attitudes toward property, in particular, do not change quickly. But the value is not in the property. We overemphasize its condition, when the problems are far deeper. Anyone who has watched the flower gardens grow in a housing project and seen fewer of them destroyed each successive year can sense that change comes only gradually and without pressure.

In many cases, what is viewed as "vandalism" of park facilities is actually the designer's fault, because of constructions that are underdesigned or overprecious. A destroyed design is one   *149* that wasn't strong enough to withstand the rigors and inventiveness of children's play. In the Quincy Street treehouse, for instance, nails holding the too-small 2x4s came loose, and when the children saw this opening, they lost no time in testing their strength on the rest of the structure.

But the myth holds the community responsible: "If they can't take care of it, they don't deserve it." At Quincy and Lefferts Streets, though, it was understandable that they couldn't take care of the park: they were working. When the park deteriorated, the officials said that the community wasn't ready for it.

Residents of New York's fashionable Sutton Place are not expected to take care of a local facility.

Maintenance is crucial. Any public space must have an ongoing structure for maintenance. To do less is to do a disservice to designer and community alike.

Jobs as a Catalyst

The catalyst for change in a community is decent wages through meaningful jobs. Employment can help a community to change itself. The real goal in building a vest pocket park is to build the human resources in the community, not just the physical resources.

But all too often, self-help programs are paternalistic and infuriating. One technique, for instance, is to give a community a carload of secondhand timbers, pay persons who are otherwise unemployed a meager dollar or so an hour, and expect them to develop pride

in their labor and respect for their achievement.

These self-help programs have not worked. They are based on the Protestant ethic, by which moral virtue follows absolutely from hard work. But this is meaningless for a man whose work is no more and no less than his economic survival. Moral virtue has no place in the equation and only clouds the issue. If all that an unskilled worker can sell is his labor, it is criminal to ask him to *give* it away.

There are abundant indications that poor people are eager to work, that they are not unemployed by choice. Indolence is not the problem; it is poverty. But grown men should receive grown men's wages. If the labor is unskilled, train it, but even in the training program, a man must not be paid so little

that he is embarrassed or loses incentive. Building a man's dignity is more important than building a vest pocket park.

Similarly, pride and identification cannot be built with secondhand materials. If anything, a deteriorated community with deteriorated morale needs a facility that is *better* than elsewhere, unique, a place of distinction.

Training for Jobs

A training program should be a natural accompaniment to the building of a vest pocket park. Men get paid while they build, and the community gets money while its facilities are being improved. Through a chain of purchasing power, money goes first to the trainee and his family, then to local businessmen who supply his daily needs, and so on.

Training is appropriate in four areas —design, construction, maintenance, and supervision. In the design phase (evaluating a community's needs and working with the professional designers), young people will be exposed to design for the first time in their lives; ideally some of the local people can be worked into apprenticeship programs in professional offices, staying together as a group for the entire time that the park is being planned and built.

In the construction stage, another group of trainees will work under a professional in the designer's office and a foreman in the field. Three-dimensional models can bridge gaps in comprehension, helping trainees gradually to understand a set of two-dimensional drawings. The foreman grows during the building process, too, with the later possibility of going into the contracting business for himself.

Maintenance crews can include those who have gone through construction training but haven't become sufficiently adept for construction work. And finally, recreation and supervision activities are one more way of creating jobs and skills in the community, with key personnel seeking out and encouraging those young people who show talent in this direction.

Obviously a single vest pocket park built in three months cannot revitalize a community, teach and reinforce new skills, open up new jobs. A program of many parks, however, can begin to build a community. This kind of program can reverse the usual slum situation in which nothing changes, nothing is believed to be changeable, and in which a man has been told of his inadequacy in so many ways that he fulfills the prophecy by his passivity.

There are other possibilities with a vest pocket park. For children, the building of a park can be a recreational and educational activity. This may be the only construction they have witnessed in their neighborhood, during their six, eight, or ten years of life. They will be constantly at the site, interested and curious, and will be easily involved if a recreation worker or shop teacher is there to provide direction. Children will work with great enthusiasm yet channel their energy into the job with surprising neatness.

For artists, too, the vest pocket park has special meaning—the chance to have their work given a public showing. Art is too often relegated to the great downtown monuments of culture, remote from daily experience. A work of art in a vest pocket park is the antithesis of this isolation between art and everyday life. An artist should be paid for his contribution to a vest pocket park, but payment can be nominal. The work of art might best be considered as if it were an early sketch or study—not a sacred and permanent (and high-priced) work but nevertheless worthy of being enjoyed by more than the artist who created it.

Actually, a vest pocket park is only an expedient, occurring haphazardly on leftover land. It is an expedient, however, that presages a whole new urban space. To be interesting and fresh, the space must be able to change repeatedly, and the designer should seek ways to give it flexibility—with demountable systems, changing exhibits, and so on. All design is experimental. Designers make many mistakes and should be the first to say that design is not permanent and eternal. Flexibility should be built into any design, from the smallest park to the largest city.

A System of Parks

Being forced into the only land that is available, the vest pocket park may serve people far from adequately. Ideally, the vest pocket park shouldn't be located arbitrarily but should be part of a city's total open-space plan. Facilities should be planned on a block-by-block basis, with an evaluation of which ones are to last, which ones are to be considered temporary.

The isolated playground is not enough for the needs that present themselves today; instead, the community should be crisscrossed with small parks—going through from block to block, linking streets together midblock, making the neighboring streets more aware of one another as social groups. And although a single vest pocket park has enormous potential—in bringing pride, identification, money, and training to a group of people—only a *system* of small parks has the potential for more than minimal change in a neighborhood.

Recreation and Economics

For economic reasons alone, apart from other valid reasons, we cannot continue providing recreational resources in the way we have been doing. Our cities are strangling, trying to build more and more public facilities and in the process taking more and more land off the tax rolls. Cities are working themselves into a hole, having to tax more heavily, and in the process threatening to drive away the very persons whose taxes keep the city going. Federal money is the logical answer to many of the problems of the cities, but it is unlikely that the Federal Government will be fully responsive to urban needs (even if expenditures for defense should be drastically reduced). Cities must find new ways to build recreational resources—new ways to provide them in the first place, without adding to the already swollen capital budgets, and new ways to keep them in

good order without adding to the already inadequate maintenance budgets.

If the job is bigger than the resources available from federal and municipal governments, what is the answer? The answer is to recognize that our parks departments (no matter how enlightened) are anachronistic, that our ways of looking at open space in the city are similarly behind the times, that our means of developing existing space and creating new space are unimaginative, and that our so-called standards are stultifying. All these factors have a direct bearing on the economic ability of the cities to provide decent recreation for city dwellers.

A Single Agency Needed

First, the archaic parks departments. To obtain the most complete use of land consistent with good design, it is essential to avoid the duplication of effort and the redundancy of facilities that plague even the most sparsely equipped city. This duplication is unavoidable as long as one playground is designed by a parks department, another playground by a housing authority, another by a board of education, and others by private developers. Each department or developer thinks of the child as *its* child. And that child is supposed to use one facility during school hours, another after school. There are some jointly operated playgrounds; there have been cooperative efforts between the board of education and the parks departments in several cities—for instance, P.S. 166 in New York City, Buchanan in Washington, and Relief School 27 in Baltimore. But this is only a beginning; the ap-

153

proach in general is still far too departmentalized. And land, as the most precious commodity of the city, is far too valuable to be carelessly allocated or inefficiently used.

One single major municipal organization should have jurisdiction over *all* open space—all streets, all sidewalks, all playgrounds, all "plaza" space around public buildings, all setback space and parking space around all buildings. Only a single agency can handle the problem on a comprehensive basis, dealing with the real needs of the whole person instead of the artificial needs, for instance, of the child fragmented between home and school.

Only a single over-all plan can deal with the concurrent demands—some realistic, some not—being made on the city for its land. The various governmental agencies today are vying for power among themselves, feuding for funds and favors, each jealously guarding its own autonomy. The waste is double—a duplication of effort in some of the facilities, with each being planned as if it were to exist alone, and a duplication of effort in the planning itself, with staffs in different agencies doing similar or overlapping work yet with little knowledge of what their counterparts are doing elsewhere in the city.

In some parts of the city, instead of having too little open space, we have too much. Under the existing arrangement whereby each agency proceeds independently (each probably under the idea that if a little open space is good, a lot is better), we have often created environments that are inimical to human beings—bleak, inhuman, deperson-

alized. We erode not only the visual space but also the economic base, using some of the most valuable land (for example, on the north–south avenues of Manhattan) for undeveloped and unproductive open space.

To put all open-space planning in one agency is strictly an administrative move; it requires no legislation and makes no change in the individual's relationship to his government. The only ones who will object are those with vested interests in the departments as they are presently organized. Others will be able to see immediate advantages in a single agency. Without the present duplication of effort, there is the possibility of needing less money to staff the agencies themselves. And without the present duplication of facilities, there is the possibility of taking less land from the tax rolls and needing less money from capital and operating budgets.

Outmoded Sense of Property

Next, our sense of property in the city. Our whole notion of open space in the city is anachronistic. The urban resident has a proprietary feeling toward the land surrounding him, inappropriately conceiving of it as the suburbanite conceives of the land surrounding his single-family home. The open space in a suburb is private territory, an extension of the private residence; the suburbanite says, "I own this land." The city dweller has also been encouraged to think of the land around him as private: a similar zoning ordinance requires similar setbacks from neighboring property lines.

But in actual fact, the urban situation is quite different; as soon as the city dweller leaves his private apartment (or the lobby of his apartment building) he is in a *public* area. Here he is in contact with vast numbers of people, almost all of them total strangers. (This is not the case in highly homogeneous neighborhoods, where almost all persons are known to one another, where familiarity breeds intimacy, and where the street becomes a kind of communal living room.) In the typically heterogeneous neighborhood, there are unwritten rules helping a person to operate, enabling him to pursue his own affairs without encroaching physically or psychologically on the strangers around him. He keeps his distance from them, with mechanisms that do not prevail in the informal suburban situation. Suburban-

ites do not share their small plot of open space in the same way; it is quite definitely an individual territory, but it is open to all in a decidedly casual way, because those who would be "trespassing" are already familiar and are therefore welcome without invitation.

The city brownstone, designed as a single-family home, may seem to conform to the suburban image, but the brownstone has changed vastly since its origin; it is now cut up into several apartments, and its outdoor space is no longer private. And in larger urban buildings it is obvious that the required setbacks for the individual building have lost their rationale. This space does not belong to the building alone but to the whole fabric of the city.

This distinction between city and suburb is blurred, to be sure. Many suburbanites do not use the space they have, and as single-family housing is built closer together, the side and rear yards will make even less sense. Suburban residents will find an increasing need for more public space and more usable private space, as densities increase. Their concept of space will become more like that of the urban residents as populations intensify.

A Network of Spaces

The open space of a city should be designed so that it adds up to a *network of meaningful space* instead of the meaningless series of leftover parcels now disconnected in form and function from one another. The minor spaces (pedestrian walkways, plazas, malls, etc.) making up such a network could be developed entirely by private enterprise (more on this later), leaving the major spaces to be developed by municipal parks departments. (These departments would continue to exist but with clearer jurisdiction than at present.) The network would not be a park in the sense of being "green." Instead, it would include all open space—not just "park" land—that is required by city people for everyday living.

A good deal of urban space is readily available for such a network. This space already exists, as space, although it may be so fragmented or so badly used as to be unrecognizable as an asset. For that matter, space is usually conceived of in the negative—being defined as what is "left over" around the positive forms of buildings. But space is a positive thing in itself; the voids in the urban fabric should be viewed as complementary to the solids.

Developing Underutilized Space

Underutilized space can be developed in many ways; the following examples are only a beginning. The back yards of brownstones, on West 94th Street, in New York City, were once the private domain of twenty individual families. Now, with sitting and play areas, and most importantly, with access from inside and from the street (through the side yards of the high-rise project and through an arcade in the rehabilitated brownstones), a potentially wasted space is turned into an appropriately public space 200 by 60 feet. The high-rise apartments and the brownstone renovations were planned two years apart, but because work had not yet been started on the first project by the time the second

was being planned, it was possible to coordinate the open space of both projects and make the space work for both projects (and for the community at large).

Front and side yards at the Nathan Straus Houses (also in New York) were wasted space until recently; they function now as social space for adults and play space for children. The side yard is a pedestrian way that brings the project back into the community from its previous isolation.

Roads frequently outlive their original use. When a road is no longer needed for transportation, it can provide a wealth of facilities, as in the projects in Brooklyn's Bedford-Stuyvesant and in Manhattan's Lower East Side. In each case, the space draws people together in a new way and provides

recreational possibilities that would not otherwise be feasible on the limited land available in these crowded urban areas.

Housing projects have vast—and useless—expanses built into them. The park at Jacob Riis Houses was an attempt to utilize this land for much-needed facilities and to make a new environment from a previously bleak place. Much credit should be given to the New York City Housing Authority, which saw its function as a public one and therefore invited the larger public into this place. Much credit, too, is due the Astor Foundation, which saw the potential impact of this pilot project. Unfortunately, this concept that should by now be commonplace is still unique.

In commercial areas, there are parallel possibilities for using existing space to better advantage. The "5½ Way"

that was proposed for Midtown Manhattan some years ago midway between Fifth and Sixth avenues would not have taken any land off the city's tax rolls but would have coordinated private open space to give pedestrians a lively north-south promenade extending some twelve blocks. In the Bellevue South renewal plan in Manhattan, setbacks, private open space and public open space provide a network of malls, plazas and parks. In Dag Hammarskjöld Plaza near the United Nations, shopping and dining (above parking) would make this presently undeveloped park in the middle of a commercial area respond in a commercial way.

Making New Space

In addition to using existing space in new ways, new space can be created where none has been before, using the air rights over streets, railroads, parking lots, and buildings. The bridge over Amsterdam Avenue at Columbia University, for instance, connects two buildings and also creates a place that is exciting to be in, for itself. At the new Police Headquarters for New York City, the need for connecting the Municipal Building and the Police Department suggested the bridging of the street; two acres of made land are the result. Major parkways along New York's East River have been covered to make the popular Carl Schurz park and the waterfront promenade in Brooklyn Heights. In Flatbush, Brooklyn, a garage and playground close an unsightly gap in the landscape and at the same time create new space over tracks of the Long Island Rail Road. At Chat- 157 ham Towers, just below New York's Chinatown, roofing over the residents' parking makes possible a sitting area on land that would otherwise be only dead storage.

And in addition to the use of air rights, landfill is a major technique for creating new land, allowing the potential development and redevelopment of the river fronts that are a feature in almost all our major cities.

Encouraging Private Interests

It does not have to cost the city money either to improve the existing open space or to create new space. Without expecting them to turn into philanthropists, we can encourage private developers to develop small spaces and serve their own interest at the same time; with proper direction from the municipal agency, these spaces can add up to a meaningful network that serves the public interest.

The techniques are available; they only need adaptation. Tax benefits, for instance: If a developer makes a park above his parking area, he should be given a tax reduction (or even a tax exemption) on these improvements. Or floor area ratio bonuses: When front and side setbacks are too small and fragmented to be used and the only organized space turns out to be the parking lot, a builder should be able to increase his total number of units, or his coverage of the site, if he roofs his parking. He is thus given an incentive to make a meaningful open space out of what would ordinarily be a single-use space and an eyesore. Benefits accrue to all: the developer gets a bonus in the

total number of units on the site; the residents and surrounding community get a better environment; and the city gets its public facilities without spending large amounts of public money.

The economic formulas of the ordinance will have to be worked out carefully. The actual granting of allowances, however, is made only after careful investigation of an area's existing facilities, relative to its population, transportation, and other variables. A single agency with jurisdiction over *all* open space is an absolute necessity to this kind of program. The ordinance should also be written to encourage new ideas for developing new land. We live in times when it is possible to float a park out into a river, or hang a park from a skyscraper, or suspend a park across a superhighway. As far as possible, a

new administrative device should anticipate (or at least not thwart) the new technology that is part of the same world.

A city could easily enliven its open spaces, and similarly without public expense, by integrating the commercial sector into its open-space program. Leases and franchises are a relatively unused device, but through them a city could provide such activities as dining, dancing, bike rentals, zoos, nursery schools, outdoor theaters and movies, roller skating, music festivals, perhaps even car washing, in its open-space network. These ventures will have to be profitable to the developer, but they will also be profitable to the city. The income from the two restaurants at Central Park's Bethesda Fountain provides New York City with eighty thousand dol-

lars each year, and the new activity draws a far larger (and broader) population than had previously come to this part of the park. A system could easily be devised, for various activities, to allow the developer a reasonable return while permitting the facilities to be enjoyed by all. Reduced admission price is a possibility (school children already have free passes for the subway, and the elderly have reduced-price tickets at many movie theaters). Certain evenings could be entirely free. Or a limited number of admissions could be purchased by those who want a guaranteed seat and do not want to wait in line. (New York City's Shakespeare-in-the-Park has an interesting system for its paying patrons. Their seats are reserved but are scattered in various rows to avoid setting up a visible distinction between them

and the majority, who pay nothing.)

Cities would also do well to offer incentives to the private sector on the maintenance of recreational facilities, in addition to the development and operation of facilities. Local maintenance is often extremely successful, being directly answerable to the users in ways that far-off bureaucracy is not. In a number of facilities the standards of private maintenance are much higher than comparable public maintenance.

New Urban Standards

A final factor needing examination is the way in which recommended "standards" for recreation are expressed in square feet per person. We squander the land, by designing many small parks with the "proper" amount of square feet per person, instead of designing creatively to an urban situation and to the kinds of activity an urban setting is called upon to provide.

To illustrate the difference, let us look at a traditional play area of the same size as the Riis playground in New York City. The traditional playground would probably have the following standard items: six swings (with a maximum capacity, at any one time, of six children), two slides (with a total capacity of ten children), four seesaws (eight children), a sandbox (fifteen), and a monkey bar (ten). Adding some children who are just wandering around, the total at peak time is perhaps fifty to seventy-five children. Riis, however, at peak times, holds two hundred to three hundred, with each feature expanding its capacity to meet the need:

more children sit on the mountaintop, or cluster at the tree house, without exhausting the feature's possibilities for play and without forcing children to wait in turn as they would at a traditional slide or seesaw. The experiences at the two playgrounds are quite different, of course: there is little "social play" at the traditional playground (except at the sandbox), whereas at Riis almost everything is social play. But even without comparing the *quality* of the experience, Riis can handle conservatively about three times the *quantity* of children. If three times the number is possible in the square footage at Riis, a city would need only one-third as many of these play environments to serve a given population.

It will be necessary, in the years ahead, to develop considerable land for open space and recreation—if people are to stay in the city and enjoy it, if they are to have even the minimal possibilities for healthy play. But by following the National Recreation Association's standards of square footage per person, we will no longer have a city, we will have a suburb. We must develop more open space, but it should be developed in ways appropriate to the number of people that urban densities deliver. This approach will help preserve the urban fabric in its visual sense, keeping the city as the tight-knit environment that is its special excitement. It will also help preserve the economic fabric of the city, insuring that the space taken for recreational facilities is serving the maximum number consistent with decent and imaginative design.

Play and Interplay

The preceding sections of this book have concentrated on the recreational needs of different age groups. Parallels have emerged, suggesting that the concept of interplay applies to all age levels: for the child, there is interplay between play and learning; for the teen-ager, interplay between the various aspects of his developing life; for an adult, interplay between his several roles vis-à-vis family and others; and for the elderly person, interplay between his leisure activities and his need for a life of continued usefulness. "Play" is linked to many other parts of a person's life.

We have looked at these age groups, thus far, as if they existed in isolation from one another, although the urban situation clearly does not put people in compartmentalized and well-delineated groups. Urban open space (which, in its compactness and public nature, is dif-ferent from suburban open space) forces interaction across all boundaries of age, color, and creed and ethnic and economic groups. This richness of many people—and many kinds of people—is, for some, the city's greatest resource and its most compelling magnetism. The city is a place for a rich interplay among people, a place in which a variety of people mingle as one community.

It should be obvious that not all city dwellers are enamored of the city; because the very poor and the new urban minorities are almost totally excluded from the suburbs, their residence in the city cannot be considered a positive choice. And among those who choose to live in the city, one can only guess at the multiplicity of their reasons. At least some of the reasons, however, would seem to stem from the sheer diversity that makes possible the city's broad range of jobs, opportunities, art forms, ideas, and experiences.

Thus there is an inevitable *interplay among people,* and to see its fullest potential realized, we must consider basic questions about this kind of interplay. How does the child of one age, for instance, relate to children of another age? In what ways does the juxtaposition of people, of whatever age, heighten their experiences, and in what ways does it make for mutual harm? Concerning ethnic and racial integration, in what ways can an open society be furthered, providing equal access to common resources, without compromising the integrity and heritage of any single group? Concerning economic integration, in what ways can varied life styles be recognized, without perpetuating some of the worst stratifications in the society? There will be many other questions, all concerned, however, with the general question: What are the positive aspects of a "successful" interplay among people, and what are the potentially negative factors?

There is also *interplay among facilities*. In what ways can the juxtaposition of certain facilities make possible a greater benefit than would be realized by their separation? In what ways does the juxtaposition of other facilities have a negative or neutral effect? Putting a garage next to a library, for instance, does not do much for either facility. But the sequential alignment of school, library, park, dining, shopping, and rapid transit facilities can set up a positive interplay among these facilities. Most sequences are neither linear nor sequential; they have inner patterns and crosslinks that defy simple, linear arrangement. The important point is that the proximity of any two facilities sets up a dynamic that can work either for or against each of them. (And the problem is of course compounded for a real world that includes many facilities.) Furthermore, the ways in which we combine facilities can lead to the creation of new institutions—the school, for instance, can be broadly conceived as the neighborhood center (education during the day, with the school library, gym, auditorium, classroom and playground serving the neighborhood, after school, in the evenings and weekends). The form of the schoolhouse will change, depending partly upon its location, population profile, open space, and the day-to-day activity of the larger community.

The *interplay among spaces* must be considered, too—the contrasts between major and minor spaces, closed and open, formal and informal, symmetrical and asymmetrical. Any space is conditioned not only by the structures impinging on it but also by the spaces around it. The behavior of people in a space—how they move through it, how it affects them—is a product of both the buildings and the spaces.

Interplay between spaces and facilities poses another series of questions. What are the spaces that make a facility work best? (A department store needs to be located at a gathering place, an entry point, while a specialty store needs to be located on a narrow conduit.) What are the kinds of open spaces necessary for different kinds of gatherings—intimate groupings, local meetings, mass

rallies? What are the effects of different spaces on the same facility—corner location, for instance, as opposed to mid-street location for a small neighborhood park? What, in short, are the spaces catalytic to different facilities and best geared to their most effective working?

But ultimately, the *interplay among spaces, facilities, and people* should be the primary focus. Unfortunately, each of these three components is still being considered apart from the others, and in the narrowest terms.

A Pedestrian-Oriented City

If the city were truly to serve people— and be based on the interplay among spaces, facilities, and people—it would offer an entirely different kind of environment. As a primary necessity, it

would be crossed with networks of pedestrian-oriented experiences. People would be separated from the indignities and dangers of open competition with vehicles. Vehicles would be available, of course, but not on today's basis of expediency, stress, and chaos. Separation between pedestrians and transportation is not a new idea, yet we have never moved far in the direction of attaining it. Now, with enormous urban redevelopment (and new development) ahead, this separation becomes more readily possible.

A pedestrian conduit ideally would have commercial, recreational, and civic activities keyed to one another in a reciprocal form; theaters would be here, and restaurants, bars, billiard parlors, libraries, dance halls, and art galleries. Community centers would be here too, and schools, playgrounds, and churches. The corridors would be promenades, with people gathering to walk or just to sit and watch; continuous movement and activity would make these promenades simultaneously exciting and safe. This becomes a natural place for the rapid transit station, and around it the plaza that is a major part of the urban park system. Cafes and other privately operated activities fill some of the open spaces.

Pedestrian enclaves take many forms —some multilevel, going over streets, and some in streets closed to traffic. Some can be carved out of the under-developed grounds of housing projects; some can be built new. The specific form and content are not so important as the essence: this is a place where various people can find their separate enjoyment and where there is also interplay among people of all kinds.

It is obvious that the city already offers some of its richest experiences to people who come together in its public places (New Yorkers recall with pleasure and wonder the first "Be-In" taking place in Central Park several years ago). Shopping areas with space for gathering and for other-than-commercial activities are unquestionably more stimulating than undifferentiated shopping areas. Public corridors with a modulation of their own, and events of their own, cause new things to happen and enable the urban experience to attain its fullest potential for all participants.

Interplay at All Levels

The proposed state park for the Bronx side of New York's Harlem River is an example of these concepts of interplay. (The project will generate a new park and community from land that is now inaccessible, underutilized, and marred by industrial blight. New housing will be built, without relocation, on a platform using the air rights over existing transportation arteries.) The project will, first of all, foster interplay among people. There will be a wide choice in recreation for each person and for the family as a unit. There will also be interplay between the community and the city at large: people from the rest of the city are expected to come here by public transportation; and a pedestrian link connects the park to Manhattan over the river by tramway and back to the Bronx by bridges and decks.

Supporting this interplay among peo-

ple, there will be interplay among facilities.' Shopping will be located at the transportation station; the school will relate logically to park and residential areas; housing will be located amid the parkland. (Transportation within the park will be handled by a minibus system, supplementing rapid transit from outside and complementing the needs of the person on foot.)

The project will also be built on an interplay among spaces. Open space will penetrate and unite all areas—residential, commercial, educational, recreational. The open space will do more than ameliorate a blighted strip at the river edge; it will permeate the entire development. Since all open space is under a single agency, it is possible to achieve a more unified framework for the space, and a more rational use of it (the community at large, for instance, will use the same sports fields as the schools). The entire project will be developed by the state, under its new State Park Commission in concert with the Urban Development Corporation, although it could have been developed privately.

It is difficult to say, with these levels of interplay, whether the park surrounds the community or the community *is* the park. The complete proposal can be thought of as a way of simultaneously bringing public open space to people and of placing people in public open space. It is unusual in that it locates a state park in a dense urban setting, and probably more unusual in trying to make these facilities serve the whole man and the whole community. It is no longer the "facilities" approach, fragmenting the person and fragmenting the community, but an approach recognizing the various levels of interplay that can make the urban experience a rich one.

Prerequisites of Change

We lack neither money nor ideas for improving the environment; we lack initiative. We are stifled by a public system that deals only with emergencies and rarely makes a significant step toward solving the larger problems. City government provides the minimal facilities it can get away with—the least it can offer without incurring unmanageable hostility or awkward political repercussions. Progress is usually geared to profit; all else operates on an archaic and patchwork level. The few good things in any city are often the result of private money and the interest of private citizens working almost in spite of the public agencies. In the face of inactivity and insufficiency, residents become inured to life itself, apathetic to gross indignities, "satisfied" with very little, seemingly glad to have the meanest facilities. In the face of lack of pressure, city government tends to continue dealing only with the immediate.

Examples of lost opportunities are numerous, and one wonders what it will take to increase the proportion of wins to losses. For one thing, it will take a belief that the city can be more amenable to urban residents than it now is and that urban residents must share in the responsibility of making it so. The professional designer can only give guidance—and perhaps agitation; the citizen's role is the vital one of exerting pressure and exercising civic power.

Our attitudes concerning open space must change. Open space is not for leftover space, and recreation is not for leftover time.

Our passivity must change. The city is becoming steadily more hostile to human beings, both physically and psychologically, and we do little to change the trend or even protest against the worst offenders. It is argued that zoos are more carefully designed than cities. Our very adaptability acts against us: if we were wilder animals, we would waste away and die; instead, we adjust, and do not measure the toll that the environment exacts.

Our automatic reliance on the "tried and true" must change. We must revise the organizational structure by which the recreational environment is designed, developed, and managed. A single agency for all open space in a city is essential. We must avail ourselves of all the potential we have—the technical know-how, the governmental mechanisms, the economic incentives—to create new ways of improving the environment. Space is too precious to waste. Lives are too precious to waste.

A Beginning

The projects that follow, designed by M. Paul Friedberg & Associates, illustrate the book's basic philosophy—that the designer must understand the genuine needs of people, that government must change its priorities and policies to reflect these needs, and that a more human use of space can be made only if users, designers, and government act in concert toward that end.

Unquestionably, the need for more recreational places is increasing as recreation becomes increasingly significant. But the available space is all around us, too. The most obvious and perhaps most important point about these projects is that they came from left-over space: an unused sideyard, a dreary housing project mall, a barren schoolyard, a garbage-strewn lot. The list goes on: *every* city can look to its streets as the single most neglected source of available open space; *every* city has its "liability" parks offering little recreation in return for the maintenance required; *every* city ignores its riverfront.

Space *is* available; it is just not being used to meet people's needs. These needs are not simple, of course. The concept of "interplay," as developed in this book, suggests that planning should recognize the complexity of the urban population and answer simultaneously the multiple needs of different people and the multiple needs of each person. "One-dimensional design"—a term used without kindness—is the flattening out of all "extra" dimensions and unexpected possibilities in a person or community.

Interplay is organic in those parts of our cities that have grown up over the years and are adaptable to varied use by varied people. Only our newer attempts at city building and rebuilding lack any sense of interplay—the downtown plazas with nothing happening (or meant to happen) to people as they scurry across a wind-swept expanse, or the housing projects with nothing but housing (and that for only one kind of person, the outcast poor).

The final project in this book is grounded in interplay—interplay between recreation and housing, between young people and old, between active and passive, between resident and visitor. The reclamation of American cities must not replace urban richness (or barrenness) with one-dimensional monotony, but must create new places of vitality, complexity, possibility—interplay. The projects that follow are an attempt at a beginning in this direction.

Nathan Straus Houses discard the idea of private space around apartment towers in favor of public use of the space and an environment that respects and strengthens the city fabric. A widened sidewalk which includes the front yard makes a significant area; a canopy of trees gives emphasis and shade. Play areas are within view of sitting areas for interplay between age groups.

Carver Houses explore new uses for the coercive "don't touch" space of a housing project. Paths were eliminated to provide freedom of movement, and seating was made for groups instead of loners. Walls and trellises sculpt a variety of "rooms." Terraced steps handle the steep drop and make an amphitheater. The place is permissive and treats people as human beings.

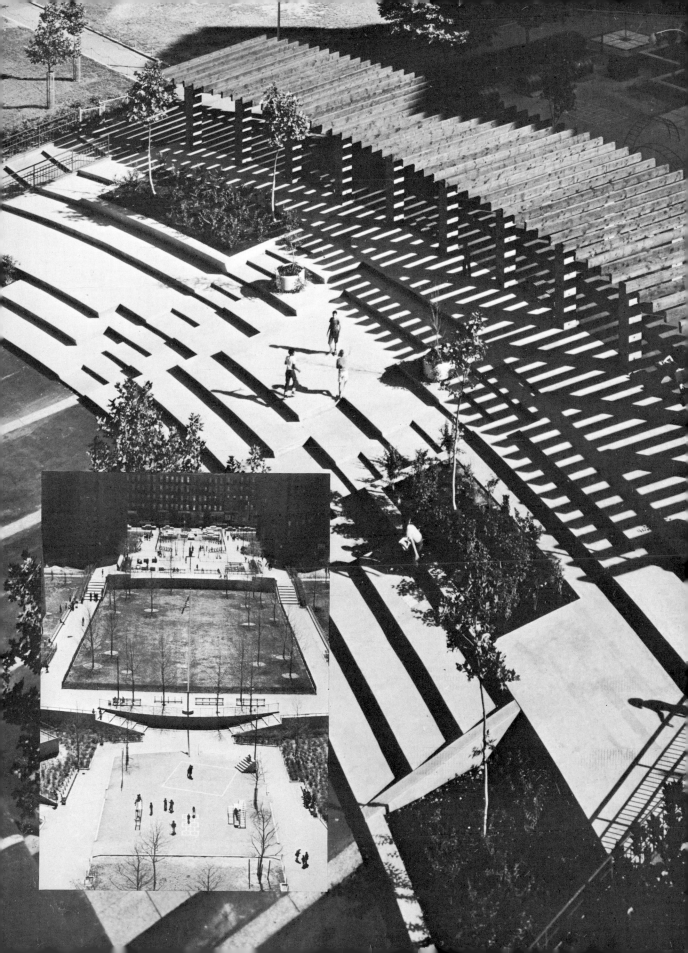

Riis Houses continue the attempt to bring new life to a housing project's proprietary dead space, creating an environment of such attraction in the neighborhood that it destroys the image of the "project" as turf to be avoided. From top to bottom: an enclosed "garden" abandoned by the elderly but taken over by teen-agers hungry for privacy; an amphitheater serving as play space, theater, spray pool, or sitting area; a plaza for checkers or quiet socializing; a playground where play is more than just a physical exercise.

Riis Houses—The playground makes play a challenging and creative process; the amphitheater brings 1000–1500 people a night into a place that had been desolate, forbidding, and dangerous.

Buchanan School changes the traditionally isolated and undeveloped schoolyard into a rich focus for the whole community. A variety of experiences is offered to the community at large and to the students at Buchanan. A basketball court is depressed in elevation instead of being surrounded by chain-link fencing. The area doubles as spray pool and dance floor and is buffered from the street by snack bar, office, and comfort station. An adults' sculpture and sitting plaza is in close visual and physical contact with the children's play area.

P.S. 166 transforms another dismal and inadequate schoolyard into a community facility. It is different from Buchanan, serving a more local population and a smaller age range (five to twelve). Also, large-scale facilities were not needed with Central Park nearby. The comfort station is below the slide mound to save space. Unfortunately, integration of the playground with the rest of the neighborhood was prevented by a fence, installed at the insistence of the school authorities.

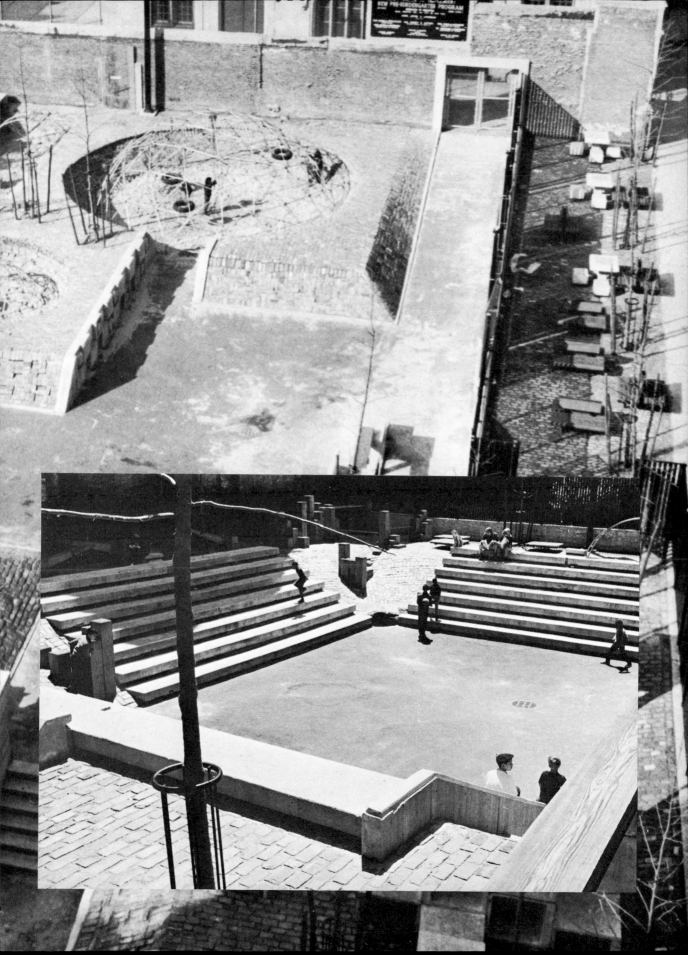

Vest Pocket Parks use garbage-laden empty lots for the everyday recreation of the very young and very old. Some conclusions from our experience: second-hand materials are inappropriate for a run-down neighborhood, single parks are best linked in a larger system, and communities can, through training programs, rehabilitate their physical and economic situations.

Experimental Systems explore the use of modular design for playgrounds since custom-design cannot produce the massive number of necessary playgrounds. Four modular designs were developed, each with mass-producible components: 1) tubular steel bars, 2) concrete U- and J-shapes, 3) pipe and cable units, and 4) stacked timbers. As if building with blocks, the designer or community can use the components to create any desired, overall form. The equipment is easily dismantled for removal to another site or for adjustment to new needs. Since no footings are required, no part of the installation is ever wasted.

29th Street Vest Pocket Park, with Nature Study Center could be a way for the urban dweller to keep in contact with nature. The small nature study center, although ultimately not built here, could have found many local users as a one-of-its-kind facility. Linked to a total plan for nature study throughout the city, and sharing personnel and resources, it could have been even more meaningful. This particular center was designed to be below grade, leaving the surface for play. It has a small planetarium, rudimentary lab space, and place to display and store the children's work.

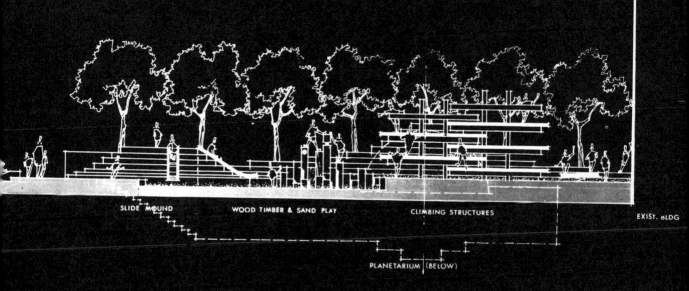

SLIDE MOUND   WOOD TIMBER & SAND PLAY   CLIMBING STRUCTURES   EXIST. BLDG

PLANETARIUM (BELOW)

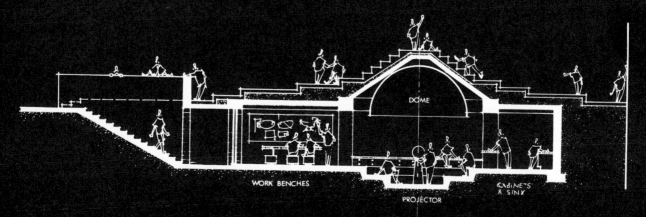

WORK BENCHES   DOME   CABINETS & SINK   PROJECTOR

planetarium

Riis-Tompkins Link was to be a project recognizing that many streets already have social and recreational value and are not fully needed for traffic. This project would also have linked two major urban spaces, Riis Houses and Tompkins Square Park. Parking would have been handled on empty lots, perhaps depressing the parking half a level below the street and using the roof decks (half a level above the street) for active play.

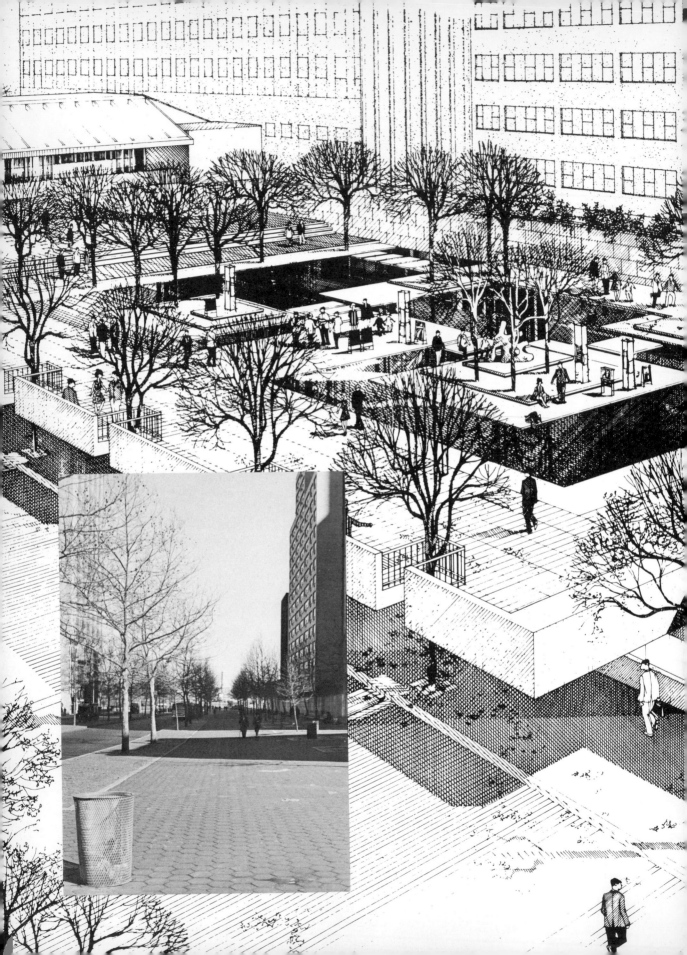

Dag Hammarskjold Plaza was planned to transform an underused park into a self-supporting attraction. A unique location, near the UN, suggested a unique treatment with sidewalk cafe, exhibition area and film library for those visiting and working in the area. Since a highway enters the city a few blocks away, a garage would be an ideal income-producing adjunct.

Harlem River Bronx State Park
will be a city in a park, a park in
a city. This site had turned its back
on the river. Housing seemed the best
way to provide a bridge between the
existing community and the riverbank.
Two state agencies are now involved,
and housing will be built along with
the park—in fact, *inside* the park.
New housing will utilize air rights
over the Major Deegan Expressway
and the Penn-Central tracks; hence,
no relocation is necessary. Interplay
between recreational, residential, educational, and commercial uses marks
the beginning of a new urban planning.

Harlem River Bronx State Park is not a Radiant City approach with towers in a vast green space. The fabric will be quite urban—the hard surfaces of an urban landscape, the high density of an urban center, and the rich interplay of many people and many activities that are the essence of the urban experience.